Wade Fishing the Rappahannock River of Virginia

Smallmouth Bass and Shad

By Steve Moore

Dedication

To **Carl Craig**, the owner of Fly Fishing Benefactors, who, unlike the Grinch whose heart is two sizes too small, his is two sizes too big. Not only does he design and manufacture a great line of fly fishing gear, but he gives away most of the profit to support fishing causes like Project Healing Waters, Casting for Recovery and others. My gratitude extends also to his wife, Emily, who tolerates his fishing obsession and allows him to hang out with guys like me.

To **Jamie Gold**, my volunteer editor and enthusiastic smallie hunter, who gives up his free time to drag through my rough drafts in a valiant attempt to protect my limited reputation as a writer.

Copyright Calibrated Consulting, Inc, 2011

Exclusive of underlying Government maps, extracts from federal, state and county regulations, the Virginia Department of Game and Inland Fisheries Phelps WMA map, other public domain material and the content of the Outfitter chapter extracted from websites owned by the businesses profiled that was either quoted or paraphrased. Google, LL Bean, Bass Pro Shop, Gander Mountain, Orvis, TFO, Fly Fishing Benefactors are the trademarks of the respective companies and the use of those names does not constitute an endorsement of this book.

Published by Calibrated Consulting, Inc
ISBN: 978-0-9823962-6-1 (0982396260)
Feedback: feedback@catchguide.com

Other CatchGuide books by Steve Moore:

Wade Fishing the Rapidan River of Virginia
From Smallmouth Bass to Trout
The Confluence to Skyline Drive

Wade and Shoreline Fishing the Potomac River for Smallmouth Bass
Chain Bridge to Harpers Ferry

Trout and Smallmouth Fishing on the North Branch of the Potomac
A Western Maryland River

Wade Fishing the Rappahannock River of Virginia   The CatchGuide Series

Steve Moore
The SwitchFisher- Bass or Trout... it is all good!
Fishing the North Branch of the Potomac

Steve is an avid, hard-core, terminally addicted fisherman. He was ruined for life when his father introduced him to the sport at the age of 7 while living in Norway as a result of military duty. Chasing trout on mountain streams left an enduring imprint and drive to find new water... something that tortures Steve to this day.

Of course, this was preordained since Steve's father was fishing in a local bass tournament on the morning he was born. He claims to have had permission to go, but Steve's mother does not remember the actual facts matching that story. The point that he won a nice Shakespeare reel did nothing to mitigate the trouble he was in upon his return.

Liability Disclaimer and Warning: It goes without saying that *fishing in rivers is dangerous* and that is particularly true of this river as a result of the fast water, deep potholes and slick rocks that occur at random, unexpected places. You need to exercise caution, particularly in the spring when the water is high, before you fish anywhere. *You should always wear a life vest* when fishing. In addition, a wading staff will help you keep your balance as you walk down the shoreline or wade in the river. There are also wild animals, such as bears, that you must be prepared to encounter.

Even when you take all precautions, you can still be severely injured. The bottom line is that you must make your own judgment in terms of acceptable behavior and risk and not rely on the **opinions** contained in this book. The regulations governing legal access to the river may change at any time and it is **your responsibility to understand the law.** *The discussions in this book are opinions and are not legal advice.* Nothing in this book should be construed as encouraging you to trespass on private property.

The author and publisher of this book shall not be held liable in any way or manner for errors, misleading or incorrect information found in this book. If you find an error, please send an e-mail to feedback@catchguide.com and we will correct the error in the next edition. Accordingly, *the author and Calibrated Consulting, Inc disclaim all liability and responsibility for any actions you take* as a result of reading this CatchGuide.

If you do not agree with the unrestricted release from liability expressed above, you should not read this book and definitely should not take any of the advice offered here. *Use of this material is at your risk.*

Table of Contents

Introduction 7

General Perspective on the Rappahannock System 8

Rules and Regulations 10

Water Volume and Flow 17

Best Time to Fish 19

Rating Summary 21

Fredericksburg - US 1 Bridge 26

Fredericksburg - I-95 Bridge 37

Motts Run 46

Motts Run Reservoir 55

Clore Brothers 58

The Confluence 65

Richards Ferry Road - City Campsite 77

Rappahannock River Campground 83

Snake Castle Rock 96

Phelps Wildlife Management Area 107

Phelps WMA South 108

Phelps WMA Sumerduck 115

Phelps WMA Middle (Pipeline) 122

Phelps WMA Bass Pond	129
Kellys Ford	133
Hogue Tract	140
Remington	145
Lakota (Freeman Ford)	153
Springs Road (VA 802)	157
Warrenton - Lee Highway	162
River above Lee Highway	168
Shad!!	174
Gear Guide	180
Outfitters	186
Water Flow - Fredericksburg	192
Water Flow - Remington	193
Water Temperature	194

Introduction

This is the fourth book in the CatchGuide series and it remains true to the core purpose – to be the ultimate reference for those who fish on their feet. That said, canoe and kayak enthusiasts will find the discussion of the various access points informative, providing additional insight on where they can enter and leave the river.

For the wading angler, I cover 24 access points and the adjacent 42 miles (approximate) of fishable river on the Rappahannock between the US 1 Bridge in Fredericksburg all the way up to Chester Gap at the eastern edge of the Blue Ridge.

Relying on foot power provides an angler a colossal advantage given the ebb and flow of the river during the summer. When kayakers start doing more hiking than floating in late June as they drag their boats across the interminable shallow sections, the water is perfect for the foot-borne smallmouth hunter who uses that same shallow condition to walk quickly to the productive pools and runs. Once you wade a short distance away from the access point, you own the river.

Beyond flexibility, wading actually allows you to spend more time fishing the good spots. Once you start the long float down the river in a canoe or kayak, you are condemned to spend far more time than you like drifting over bad water or just paddling to get to the finish line. With the amount of water up or downstream from each of the access points limited only by your willingness to walk, you spend more time fishing the 10% of the water that holds 90% of the fish. Granted, a floating fisherman will be able to throw a lure in places that a wader can only dream about as a result of the barrier presented by distance and private property. But, in the long run, by following the guidance in this book, a wading angler will be able to spend more days on the river, in the right places.

Need to know where? This is the book for you.

I certainly hope you find this CatchGuide helpful and wish you the best of luck on the stream.

Steve Moore

General Perspective on the Rappahannock System

In the Algonquian Indian language, Rappahannock means "rapidly rising and falling waters" and, every Spring, the river demonstrates why the name is appropriate. During that stormy season, flood waters charge downriver with fantastic velocity and violence causing the huge spikes in turbulence that are an inescapable lure to legions of kayakers. But the name is inadequate to describe the quality and variety of the fishery that exists under its roiling surface. Although the name is unlikely to change to whatever the Algonquian translation of "angler's heaven" is, in addition to smallmouth bass, you are likely to scream a panicked "FISH ON" as massive redbreast sunfish, carp or even yellow perch and channel catfish pull hard against your smoking drag once the season drifts from frantic Spring into calm Summer.

Granted, I do not cover all 184 miles of the Rappahannock from its dim origin at Chester Gap in the Blue Ridge to the tidal flats lining the Chesapeake Bay, but I do cover the 59 (42+ wadeable) miles that represent the interesting core of the river for smallmouth bass fishing enthusiasts. Besides, below the bridge, the river runs wide, slow and sandy; becoming the domain of largemouth bass pursued by hard-eyed anglers leveraging every ounce of technology packed into supercharged bass boats.

Above the fall line, the high-powered bawl of a 200 hp Mercury engine is replaced by the quiet dip of paddles or the hushed slosh of ragged sneakers moving through the shallows. While the book is useful for kayakers and canoeists since the good places are good regardless of how you reach them, my focus is on those who fish on their feet - the sweaty grunt, the fishing infantry. The book includes the well-known angler's playgrounds at Snake Castle Rock and the Confluence - usually the restricted domains of kayakers and canoeists who reach these honey holes via a long downstream float. As I describe later, a short hike, coupled with a bit of perspiration, gives you the opportunity to fish normally inaccessible locations.

In general, what makes water good for smallmouth is structure; specifically, rocks and gravel with a dash of vegetation and fallen logs. Unlike the Rapidan, the number of access points holding good rocky structure increases the farther from the mountains the river runs, culminating in the rocky jumble upstream from the US 1 bridge. The best spots are those where a drop in elevation or a tight bend compresses the push of the water to scour the sand and reveal the bottom. If you were only to look at the river from bridge crossings, you would miss most of the excellent areas. As I fished the river, I resolved to try to wade at least a mile in either direction from each access point. In all but a few cases, I was successful in meeting that goal and, in the process, discovered the magic 10% of the water that holds 90% of the fish. The maps and GPS coordinates I include provide a perspective on where those locations are so you can judge your physical ability to reach them. In addition, you may want to go beyond where I ended (or at least ended discussion for this book). It was not my intent to walk every mile of the river.

In addition to the 23 maps, this book includes 279 GPS coordinates. Use that information to preview the river. The coordinates are in a format compatible with Google Maps, and in the eBook version, each coordinate is a clickable link that instantly opens the satellite view of that location. If you zoom in on a particular spot, you can assess the density of the rocks, and the associated structure to make your own call in terms of whether it is "worth it." One caveat on the satellite picture - Google updates the satellite view periodically and it is the luck of the draw on the amount of intelligence you can gain. If the picture was taken at low water during the summer, you just hit a gold mine! At high resolution, you can see the rocks under the water and, if you look closely, the darker areas show where the deep water is and the big fish lie. When you stumble upon a low, clear water picture, print it for future reference! As a purchaser of this book, the eBook is available from www.CatchGuides.com for only $7.95 using the discount code of "rapp" while the offer lasts.

Beyond the GPS coordinates, review the 252 included pictures carefully. Like the coordinates, the staggering number of pictures allows you to cast an angler's eye on the water without having to burn the fossil fuel and even more precious human energy to reach that location. Use them to assess the shoreline structure and the character of the river. Between the satellite view and the pictures embedded in the book, you should know exactly what to expect before you put your foot on the gas pedal. My descriptions and advice round out the background. If you purchase the eBook, you should print the relevant chapter and take it with you as an "on water" reference.

Three final comments:

- Even though the river is generally shallow, there are deep sections that will surprise you, particularly when the water is milky. Therefore you should exercise the appropriate caution and wear a personal flotation device (PFD) to provide protection from any surprise the river offers.
- Please reread the disclaimer and warning at the front of the book. You are ultimately accountable for what you do or fail to do on the river and I, the author, as well as the publisher and anyone else involved in the creation of this book disclaim all liability from actions you take. As stated in the disclaimer, by reading this book you agree to an unrestricted release from liability. If you cannot agree to that, then put this down right now and read something else.
- I show the GPS coordinates in a format compatible with Google Maps. To load them into your GPS, remove the "minus" sign in front of the second number. Also, when you open Google Maps using the coordinates, *you may have to zoom out until you see the GREEN arrow*. Google tends to jump to a known feature, sometimes miles away, shown using a RED arrow with a letter in the middle.

Rules and Regulations

Where can you wade? Depends. And.... that makes this the most difficult chapter of this book to write.

Sparks fly when the issue of river access comes up and the side of the argument you find yourself on usually depends on whether you own property that borders a waterway in the State. Even the professionals in the State government are reluctant to go on record with an opinion. So, now is the time to reiterate the opening disclaimer in the strongest of terms. I am not a lawyer, just a fisherman. This chapter contains my analysis of the situation that was reviewed by a number of different experts, who, for the same reason, asked that nothing be attributed specifically back to them. **Nothing in this chapter should be regarded as legal advice.** The responsibility for any decision you make based on reading this, or, for that matter, using any information in this book, is yours alone and I point you back to the unrestricted release from liability disclaimer at the front of the book.

Trespassing

Before we get to the streambed, I need to cover the more general topic of trespassing. Other authors, in other books, sometimes refer to "informal" access points along the various rivers and streams in our State. Just because a road runs next to a stream does not mean you can walk from the roadway to the stream. In most cases, that thin strip of land separating the road from the water is privately owned. An exception is the Virginia Department of Transportation (VDOT) right-of-way. The right-of-way is a public easement that authorizes anyone to travel across the land included in the easement. In fact, many of the access points in this book properly use the VDOT right-of-way associated with bridges to get you to the water without problems. Here is how VDOT describes the right of way:

Definition: *"Right-of-way" means that property within the system of state highways that is open or may be opened for public travel or use or both in the Commonwealth. This definition includes those public rights-of-way in which the Commonwealth has a prescriptive easement for maintenance and public travel. The property includes the travel way and associated boundary lines, parking and recreation areas and other permanent easements for a specific purpose. (24VAC30-151-10)*

Note that the right-of-way can either be explicit with the strip of property owned by the State or it establishes a prescriptive easement that demands the property owner recognize the public's right to use the narrow band of his or her property bordering the road. I was pleased to see that the definition mentions both parking and recreation areas; confirming that we can leave our vehicles safely parked within the boundary of the easement. So, what is the formal definition of a road? According to the statute, ""highway," "street," or "road" means a public way for purposes of vehicular travel, including the entire area within the right-of-way." Clearly, if the road is a State maintained road, the public has access to the entire area.

Size of the right-of-way: "*There is no standard right of way distance for every road. Generally, the right of way ranges from 25-150 feet from the road's center line.*" (VDOT website)

You have to talk to VDOT to determine the specific width of the right-of-way on the specific road in the specific place where you have questions. There may be some rare places where 25 feet will extend all the way to the water. If you believe you have discovered an instance where the river runs close enough to the road to be included in the right-of-way, you should discuss it with VDOT. To save you some work, I have already done the research for you regarding the Rappahannock. I only found one place where there was a potential for the easement to overlap the streambed. Since this particular location was close enough to a bridge crossing where public rights are well-established, I did not bother to mention it in the discussion since a technical argument with a landowner will not end well at the edge of the river.

That establishes where you can be, but what if there are no "no trespassing" signs? How do you know who owns that strip of land? Unless you take the time to look it up on the Internet using the Graphical Information System (GIS) for your county (http://www.gispilot.com/States/Virginia.html), you should assume that it is private property. There are rare cases when State owned land extends from the water to the road and I documented every instance in this book. For example, the Snake Castle Rock access point specifically uses the City of Fredericksburg property that borders the river. Likewise, there is public property at Kellys Ford and other places that provide access to water not associated with a VDOT easement.

It is easy to use the GIS system. Do a generic search for the name of the county and the abbreviation, "GIS" or locate it on the summary site quoted above. Follow the instructions of the website to quickly zoom in on the actual property record and discover the name and address of the landowner. Using the name, do a look up in whitepages.com if you want to ask for permission to fish. If you would like to duplicate my research to convince yourself, the Rappahannock runs adjacent to Stafford, Culpeper, Spotsylvania and Fauquier counties. In addition, Google Maps, at the most detailed resolution level, now shows property lines for many areas.

Here is how the Virginia (Section 18.2-119) defines the crime of trespassing:

"*If any person without authority of law goes upon or remains upon the lands, buildings or premises of another, or any portion or area thereof, after having been forbidden to do so, either orally or in writing... he shall be guilty of a Class 1 misdemeanor.*"

Those of you who read words closely, have probably locked in on the phrase "*after having been forbidden to do so, either orally or in writing*", immediately jumping to the conclusion that if there are no signs, then you can go anywhere you would like to go. Wrong.

Section 18.2-132 specifically targets hunters and fishers:

"*Any person who goes on the lands, waters, ponds, boats or blinds of another to hunt, fish or trap without the consent of the landowner or his agent shall be deemed guilty of a Class three misdemeanor.*"

For the curious, a Class three misdemeanor will not only earn you a criminal record, but also inflict a fine of not more than $500 on you for your carelessness. Note that this section does not discuss whether notice was posted or not. Therefore, you need to exercise the appropriate care before you wander across property to get to the river. If it is private, and you are on it, whether it is posted or not, you are trespassing. Remember that thin strip of property I mentioned above? It counts.

One final critical point about permission. The best permission to have is written permission. If a conservation police officer stops you on posted land and you claim to have verbal permission from the landowner, he will likely ask you to prove it. Your word is not good enough and you will probably get a ticket that will be dropped later once you present proof from the landowner. I doubt that a call to the landowner on your cell phone would suffice. First of all, in many of the areas discussed, cell phone coverage is spotty. Second, how does the conservation police officer know that he is talking to the actual landowner? Therefore, the next time you see your landowner friend, have him sign a short, sweet and to the point permission slip that gives you the authority to use his property. Keep it with your fishing license. See the VDGIF recommended permission form at the end of this chapter.

VDOT Bridge Right-Of-Way

Given the uncertainties associated with whether the VDOT right-of-way extends from the road to the river, we must rely on the better known, and well established, easement that surrounds most bridge crossings in the State to reach the water's edge. The Virginia Department of Game and Inland Fisheries (VDGIF) is explicit about the public's right to use this access method. For example, when discussing access to the Rapidan river on its website, it states:

"*Access may also be gained via several non established points. These consist of VDOT right-of-ways along bridges (e.g., VA 522 on the Rapidan).*"

Therefore, as long as you stay within the right of way, you can skinny down the edge of the bridge to get to the river. Obviously, this is another area of contention if the landowner is not as educated as you are on what a VDOT right-of-way is. Of all the access points I discuss in the book, there are only three where this might be a problem. Given that the fishing is unremarkable, your potential opportunity to have a discussion evaporates. Unless you are a glutton for punishment, do not go to those places.

Do not extrapolate this rule to every bridge in the State. Some bridges, especially those in the Shenandoah Valley, are privately owned and maintained. A State maintained road may not lead all the way to the bridge. If it is not a public road, there is no public right-of-way. All of the bridges discussed in this book are public with a public road running across them.

Streambed

So far, except for the key point about access near bridges, this chapter has been mostly bad news. What is a book on fishing doing spending so much time on where you cannot fish? It is important to stay legal. It is crucial to respect landowner rights or the situation worsens for all of us. If we do things to put the landowners adjacent to our State's waters up in arms, we all lose since the issue of streambed ownership is not fully settled.

What many anglers do not understand is that the simple act of walking on the streambed triggers a whole new set of cautions. As a result of a "dog's breakfast" of conflicting rules including several hundred-year-old crown grants from the King of England, acts of the State Assembly and a limited set of court decisions carefully written to prevent broad application, Virginia does not make it easy to determine who owns the streambed on our State's waterways.

While the majority of the Rappahannock and Rapidan river systems are "good to go" in terms of public use and streambed access, there are some gray areas. There is a bright dividing line on the Rappahannock. The VDGIF declared the entire streambed below US 211 outside of Warrenton as public. While the streambed at the remaining five bridge crossings above US 211 have not been declared off limits, they clearly fall into a gray area of swirling uncertainty.

To understand the shades of gray, you need to understand a little bit of the legal situation.

Virginia's declaration that the State owns streambeds can be traced to the following statute first implemented in 1780:

Section 28.2-1200. Ungranted beds of bays, rivers, creeks and the shores of the sea to remain in common.

All the beds of the bays, rivers, creeks and the shores of the sea within the jurisdiction of the Commonwealth, not conveyed by special grant or compact according to law, shall remain the property of the Commonwealth and may be used as a common by all the people of the Commonwealth for the purpose of fishing, fowling, hunting...

While this established the State's ownership of streambeds and the right of the public to use them, the alert reader has probably already focused on the subtle phrase, *"not conveyed by special grant or compact"* That is where the argument starts. Given the age of Virginia and the inducements to colonization that existed prior to the American revolution, parts of the State were conveyed to individual landowners at some point in its early history.

Most anglers in Virginia are aware of the access issues associated with the Jackson River. In 1996, the Virginia Supreme Court recognized that "kings grants" issued by Kings George II and III in 1750 and 1759 respectively gave several landowners on the upper Jackson River some control over the river where it ran through their property. As a result of those grants, the Virginia statute did not apply ("*not conveyed by special grant*"), and the landowners owned the streambed as their personal property with the right to restrict access.

While the debate is settled on the specific, small section of the Jackson were a prior grant was established, there is no current debate on either the Rapidan or Rappahannock rivers as of 2010. Based on the explicit language of the statute quoted above, the public has access to the streambed as long as it obtains access legally – no trespassing. As of the date of publication, there are no known issues associated with the streambed on either river.

After waving the red flag for the last couple of paragraphs, there is a reasonable amount of clarity over portions of both the Rappahannock and the Rapidan.

In opinions tracing back to at least Bulletin 120 (*Public Recreation on Virginia's End and Streams: Legal Rights and Landowners Perceptions*), which was published in October 1979, there are references to a VDGIF position that the Rappahannock is unequivocally public from the mouth of the river to US 211 (Lee Highway) outside of Warrenton in Fauquier County. There should be no question about any access downstream from US 211.

In addition, there was a State act regarding the Rappahannock that extends the navigation from the "... *most convenient place on tide water upwards to the highest parts practicable on the main branch and other branches thereof....*" It provided that "... *the said river and the branches thereof, and the works to be erected thereon in virtue of this act, when completed, shall forever thereafter, be esteemed and taken to be navigable as a public highway....*" another proof point that confirms that the State regards both rivers as navigable and that the beds remain the property of the Commonwealth.

Therefore, for the Rappahannock, the "gray" area is anything above US 211. The five upstream crossings beyond US 211 are all small and, unlike the Rapidan, there are no deeply rutted roads or paths leading down the side of the bridges (leveraging the aforementioned VDOT easement). Beyond that, discussions with other anglers and my visual reconnaissance from the bridge crossings is not encouraging. There simply isn't enough decent water upstream of the US 211 bridge to make it worthwhile to investigate. Therefore, in the chapter on the river above Lee Highway, I heavily caveat your ability to fish that water despite the fact that Crest Hill Road and Tapps Ford Road are well-known put-in locations for kayakers and canoeists.

A point of reference that argues the case for access above US 211 is that the reference on the VDGIF website regarding using the VDOT bridge easements discusses a bridge above the nominally designated public section below Raccoon Ford on the Rapidan; confirming that the actual, firmly public, area goes farther upstream beyond what was stated in Bulletin 120. That said, the bridge crossings above US 211 are the most vulnerable to selective interpretation regarding public access given the width of the stream at those points. I'm not really sure the width or depth matters given the first line of the statute, "*All the beds of the bays, rivers, creeks...*" Crest Hill and Tapps Ford Roads are both routinely used as canoe put-in and take-out points. Hume Road, on the other hand, is a small miserable stream where you would be hard-pressed to make even a kayak argument. Sadly, I cannot provide any better advice other than not to bother – it is not worth it to make yourself a test case.

There is a bottom line to the above discussion. As anglers, we need to respect the rights of landowners by not violating their private property. Even though we can use the streambed right now, recognize that the shoreline for most of the length of the river is privately owned. When wading, chances are you will eventually get to a place where the water is too deep to allow you to continue. If you exit the river without returning to the legal access point, you are probably trespassing on private property.

Recommended VDGIF private property permission form:

AFFIDAVIT

The person whose name and address appears on the opposite side of this form has promised to use your land for outdoor recreation in an ethical way. Please read the signed pledge on the reverse side for specifics.

In deciding whether or not to allow this person to use your property, please consider that he/she is putting his/her name and address on the line as assurance that they will abide by your wishes and conduct themselves as true sportsmen or sportswomen.

PERMISSION TO

_____
Hunt, fish, trap, camp, etc.

I hereby grant the person named on the reverse side permission to use my property for the above purpose on the following dates:

_____

Signed _____
                Landowner

Name _____
Address _____
City _____ St. ____ Zip _____
Phone (____) _____
Auto License No. _____
Driver's License No. _____

I hereby absolve the landowner of all liability for my person while engaged in recreation on his property.

Signature _____

SPORTSMAN'S PLEDGE

In return for the privilege of using private property, I agree to:

1. Respect the landowner's property, going only where he designates and assume liability for my actions and my person while on this property.
2. Take every precaution against littering and fire.
3. Obey the game, fish, and other wildlife laws.
4. Observe all safety precautions and the traditions of good sportsmanship.

Signature _____

Water Volume and Flow

Knowledge of current river conditions will save you a significant amount of frustration and heartache. The quality of the fishing comes and goes with both the amount and clarity of the water. If you know what to look for and where to check to determine the current conditions, you will avoid wasted treks in grinding traffic only to discover an unfishable situation. USGS maintains two gages (yes, they spell it "gage" instead of "gauge") to monitor the status on the Rappahannock. One is near Remington and the other is farther downstream at Fredericksburg. Use the Remington gage to assess conditions above the confluence and the Fredericksburg gage for the remainder of the river downstream.

As a general statement, to be wadeable, the flow must be far below the minimum level needed to make whitewater addicts happy. There is a great website – www.americanwhitewater.org – which the kayak crowd uses to determine put-in and take-out points and share conditions. If you use a kayak or canoe, I strongly encourage you to join by going to their website. The website has real-time river flow status color-coded based on a kayaker's point of view for different sections of the river:

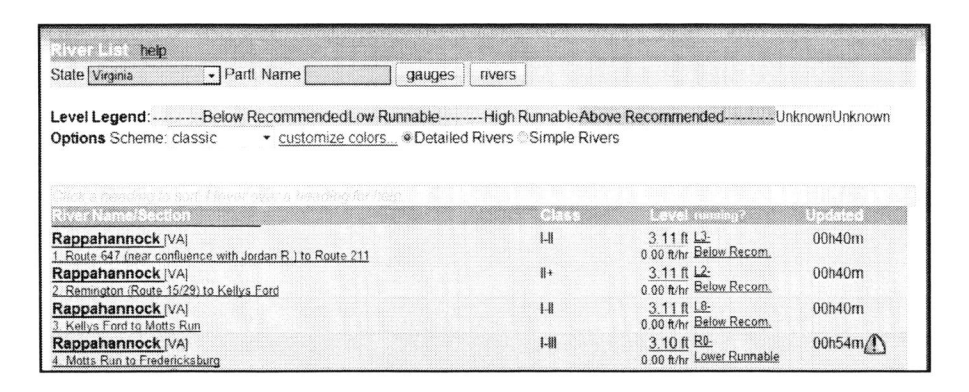

River Name/Section	Class	Level (running?)	Updated
Rappahannock [VA] 1. Route 647 (near confluence with Jordan R.) to Route 211	I-II	3.11 ft L3- 0.00 ft/hr Below Recom.	00h40m
Rappahannock [VA] 2. Remington (Route 15/29) to Kellys Ford	II+	3.11 ft L2- 0.00 ft/hr Below Recom.	00h40m
Rappahannock [VA] 3. Kellys Ford to Motts Run	I-II	3.11 ft L8- 0.00 ft/hr Below Recom.	00h40m
Rappahannock [VA] 4. Motts Run to Fredericksburg	I-III	3.10 ft R0- 0.00 ft/hr Lower Runnable	00h54m

When you click on an entry, the website provides expanded guidance on minimum/maximum whitewater levels. The gage height range that would make the trip worthwhile for a kayaker is between 4.5 and 7.0 feet on the upper Rappahannock at Tapps Ford to between 3.7 and 10.0 feet for the Kellys Ford to Motts Run float. If you are going to wade fish on the Rappahannock, even the minimum level is far above what I consider to be the maximum safe level. Therefore, all the kayak-oriented range tells you is whether you will be bothered by kayakers when you are fishing. If it is below the recommended minimum, chances are that people will not embark on the float downstream. Interestingly enough, the Virginia Outdoor Center/Friends of the Rappahannock's position is that the river is unsafe for recreational use when the river is higher than 3.2 feet at Fredericksburg. Clore Brothers agrees with the Friends while the Rappahannock River Campground only runs trips between 2.9 feet and 5.0 feet at Remington. In other words, there are plenty of opinions.

So what is the number for wade fishing? Frankly, I used to base my judgment on the gage height and used the general rule that the Rappahannock was wadeable at a gage reading of 2.41 or below at Fredericksburg. As I did the research for this book, I discovered that gage height is a poor measurement. The USGS told me that gage height is an arbitrary reading and is only used to calculate discharge. Since the river channel is dynamic and constantly changing, they correct the gage height to match current conditions. As they assess the situation, they may determine a significant change has occurred and develop a new gage height standard.

Therefore, the only reliable statistic is discharge in cubic feet per second. Unlike the North Branch of the Potomac where there is consensus and collective wisdom regarding safe wading levels associated with cubic feet per second, there is no similar body of knowledge for the Rappahannock. So, use my experience as a yardstick and, as you fish the river, make your own judgments. In the pictures associated with each access point, I usually document the discharge volume associated with that visit. You can throw your eyeball on the picture, assess the water and decide.

Above the confluence, I have not had problems wading at Kellys Ford and other places at levels of 400 cfs on the Remington gage, although the comfortable level is much lower - 300 cfs. Below the junction, the maximum I ever encountered is 2,490 cfs during shad season on the Fredericksburg gage. BUT... shad season is a different animal since wading is usually around the US 1 bridge or fishing from the shore. During the shad run, the river is very, very dangerous and you must wear a PFD.

During the normal season for bass, my maximum Fredericksburg gage reading is 1,050 cfs - and even then, it is situational. Do not try that level anywhere the river is compressed. If you go to a wide spot, like the confluence, it is fine.. with caution. **My preferred level is 450 cfs and below**. Sadly, until we gather more data, you must make your own judgment. Never, never step into the river - regardless of the gage reading - if it does not look safe. How do you know? If you cannot see the bottom to visually verify the depth.... do not fish. If you step into the river and it feels like it is going to rip your feet out from under you or if you find yourself relying on your wading staff to move - GET out! If you have a doubt about safety, then there is no doubt at all. If the river is running fast below the confluence, go farther upriver until you find a safe level.

In addition to making sure the discharge volume is at the appropriate level given your physical capability, you must consider recent rainfall. Given the extent of the drainage area feeding water into the Rappahannock system, a small amount of rain can blow out the river - something that the kayakers look forward to, but will keep a wading angler off the river. A rule of thumb is that it takes at least three days after a heavy rain for the water levels to drop back to normal.

Best Time to Fish

When to fish for bass is driven more by the water level than by temperature since the ebb of the Spring floods will occur after the temperature spurs the bass back into action. But, temperature is still important. Since there is no active temperature gage on either the Rapidan or Rappahannock, I use the Potomac as a surrogate. The Little Falls gage still provides temperature readings that correlate loosely with what you can expect on the Rappahannock. Once the temperature reading inches above 50°, the threshold for spawning, I start to get interested in the water levels. As a side note, the Rappahannock runs around 3° colder throughout the year than the Rapidan. Use that temperature difference to pick which river to visit during the transitional seasons.

In effect, the Rapidan will "light up" first for bass fishing as the temperature breaks through the 50° mark and stays active a little farther into the full feeding frenzy season. But, in the dog days of summer, the Rappahannock is the right place to go when the air temperature becomes oppressively hot.

From a temperature perspective, a Rappahannock smallmouth starts to move in mid-April, but the water volume usually remains above 400 cfs (Remington) and 1,050 cfs (Fredericksburg) until late May or early June depending on the intensity of the Spring rains. Do not be fooled. The Rappahannock can surge; becoming life-threatening very quickly. In addition, with all the Spring rain, you can count on the Rappahannock to remain clouded until the intensity and frequency of the storms abate. As with any smallmouth river, there is a significant danger wading when you cannot see the bottom. Since the water is cold until mid-June, you will undoubtedly wear chest waders that increase your opportunity to drown as a result of a careless step into a deep hole. If you decide to abandon the trout to go for early season smallmouth, be sure you wear a PFD!

On the good news front, since March, April and May are in the middle of trout season, there are few anglers working the lower river during those months. Those who do are usually kayakers or canoeists who take advantage of the high water to make the run to the Clore Brothers landing or the Virginia Outdoor Center. The result is that you should have plenty of solitude at many of the locations. Given the distance between put-in and take-out, floating fisherman rarely have the opportunity to dwell long in a single place.

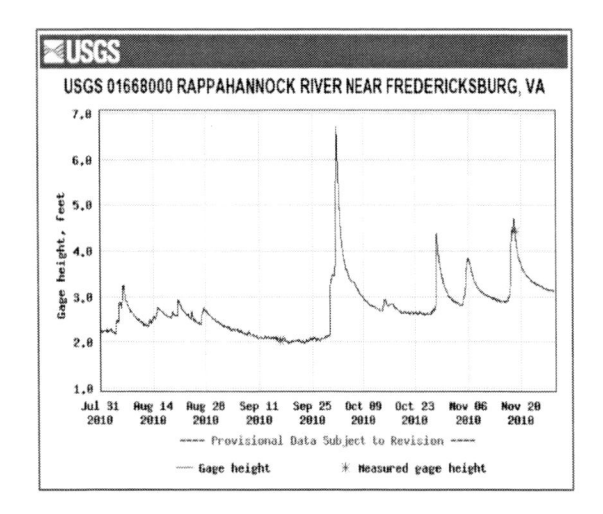

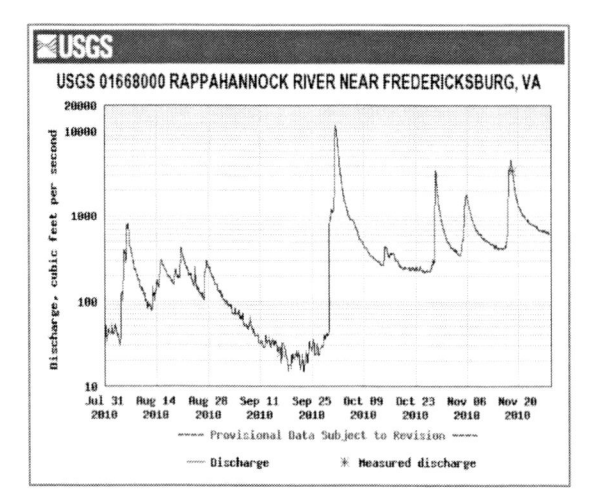

This USGS graph shows how quickly the conditions can change. Between September 27 and October 4, the river jumped almost five feet in depth.

During the same period, the volume of water pouring down the river spiked at over 11,000 CFS! Even a PFD would not keep you safe in conditions like this.

Your first opportunity to wet wade will not be until early June when the water temperature punches through the 70° mark - but it doesn't really get comfortable until July when it claws up towards 80°. At the other end of the calendar, the action dies off in mid-October when the temperature dips below 60°. Joyfully, this correlates perfectly with the restart of trout season. If you want to avoid disturbing the mountain trout, Virginia, Maryland and West Virginia all begin their fall stocking programs in mid-October. Good stocked trout water near the Rappahannock includes the Rose, Robinson and Hughes Rivers. So, there are always fish to catch!

Once you rationalize the water temperature, recognize that the gage readings are rough measurements of safety. The specific level at the various access points is driven by the physical geography at that particular place. Therefore, where the river is wide, the depth and associated impact of the water volume will be less (easier to wade) and vice versa.

All that goes to say that the best time for smallmouth fishing is between early June and late September.

Rating Summary

Understanding the Rating System

Every angler looks at a body of water in a way that matches his background and compares what he sees to his personal concept of "perfect." I am no different. To fully understand the comments I make in this guide, you need to understand how I evaluate water.

The tables below attempt to normalize my perspective into a common frame of reference. The key ratings are the ones related to physical fitness, the presence of smallmouth structure, and pressure.

The one rating that I do not include is whether fishing a particular section is dangerous. While I will point out the hazards that were apparent to me, for obvious reasons associated with liability, *you must be the final arbiter on whether you are comfortable fishing in a particular location and must use your common sense based on the conditions on that particular day prior to entering the water. You are solely and fully responsible for any decision you make to enter the river.*

The physical fitness rating is based on my impression of what it takes to get to the fishing area and enjoy it. Something I consider challenging may be easy for you or, on the other end of the scale, impossible based on your personal physical situation. *You should never attempt to fish in any spot where taking a step off the bank creates personal risk.* Just because I did not think a particular place was overly taxing physically may not mean much until you match your abilities with mine.

Please re-read and agree to the liability disclaimer at the front of the CatchGuide before you read further.

The tables below lay out the criteria:

Rating Explanations		
Parking	Green	Formal parking area with plenty of spaces
	Yellow	Informal parking area off the main road
	Red	Park on the side of the road
Canoe or Kayak Launch	Green	Access point useable by canoes or kayaks; short portage from the parking area
	Yellow	Useable but requires a carry
	Red	No easy access to launch a canoe or kayak - long walk or no path
Distance to River	Green	Parking area is next to the river
	Yellow	Short walk of less than 1/2 mile
	Red	Walk of more than 1/2 mile
Can Bike to River	Green	Using a bike would be useful and is permitted
	Red	Bike not permitted, not useful or not needed
Physical Fitness	Green	Smooth flow, easy wading, stable bottom
	Yellow	Some rock ledges, moderate water speed
	Red	Caution - fast water, slippery rocks or both
Scenery	Green	Steep cliffs, riffles, or grass beds
	Yellow	Flat water, broad sweep of river
	Red	Populated

Rating Explanations		
Spin Fishing	Green	No problems using spin gear
	Yellow	Structure may cause hang ups
	Red	Water limits use of spin gear (short shallow pools, etc)
Fly Fishing	Green	Open terrain allows backcast
	Yellow	Some obstructions for backcast
	Red	Tight vegetation; No room for backcast
Structure	Green	Rocks, ridges, grass islands that channel a moving current
	Yellow	Mix of rocks, ridges and sand; slower current
	Red	Sand everywhere
Wading	Green	Can wade without restriction
	Yellow	Can wade with limitations
	Red	Limited wading - deep water close to access point
Pressure	Green	Likely to see few other people
	Yellow	Will see other people, but will not feel pressured
	Red	Very popular location; typically crowded
Overall	Green	Always a good choice
	Yellow	A good choice if you do not have anywhere better to go
	Red	Not worth the time or the gas

Overall Rating Summary

The following two tables consolidate all of the ratings in one place for your reference.

	Parking	Boat Launch	Distance to River	Can Bike to River	Physical Fitness	Scenery
Fredericksburg - US 1 Bridge	Green	Yellow	Green	Red	Yellow	Red
Fredericksburg - I-95 Bridge	Green	Red	Red	Green	Yellow	Green
Motts Run	Red	Green	Green	Red	Yellow	Green
Motts Run Reservoir	Green	Green	Green	Red	Green	Green
Clore Brothers	Green	Green	Green	Red	Green	Yellow
The Confluence	Red	Red	Red	Green	Red	Green
Richards Ferry Road	Red	Red	Red	Green	Yellow	Green
Rappahannock River Campground	Green	Green	Yellow	Red	Yellow	Green
Snake Castle Rock	Red	Red	Red	Red	Red	Green
Phelps WMA South	Green	Red	Red	Green	Red	Yellow
Phelps WMA Sumerduck	Green	Red	Red	Green	Red	Yellow
Phelps WMA Middle (Pipeline)	Green	Red	Red	Green	Red	Yellow
Phelps WMA Bass Pond	Green	Yellow	Green	Red	Green	Yellow
Kellys Ford	Green	Green	Green	Red	Yellow	Green
Hogue Tract	Green	Red	Yellow	Green	Red	Green
Remington	Yellow	Yellow	Yellow	Red	Red	Red
Lakota (Freeman Ford)	Red	Green	Green	Red	Green	Yellow
Springs Road (VA 802)	Red	Green	Green	Red	Green	Red
Warrenton - Lee Highway	Yellow	Green	Green	Red	Green	Green

Here are the remaining ratings and an overall summary assessment for each location:

	Spin Fishing	Fly Fishing	Structure	Wading	Pressure	Overall
Fredericksburg - US 1 Bridge	Green	Green	Green	Green	Red	Yellow
Fredericksburg - I-95 Bridge	Green	Green	Green	Green	Green	Green
Motts Run	Green	Green	Green	Green	Red	Yellow
Motts Run Reservoir	Green	Green	Red	Red	Yellow	Yellow
Clore Brothers	Green	Green	Yellow	Green	Red	Yellow
The Confluence	Green	Green	Green	Green	Yellow	Green
Richards Ferry Road	Green	Green	Green	Green	Yellow	Green
Rappahannock River Campground	Green	Green	Green	Green	Yellow	Green
Snake Castle Rock	Green	Green	Green	Green	Green	Green
Phelps WMA South	Green	Green	Yellow	Green	Green	Green
Phelps WMA Sumerduck	Green	Green	Red	Green	Green	Red
Phelps WMA Middle (Pipeline)	Green	Green	Red	Green	Green	Yellow
Phelps WMA Bass Pond	Green	Yellow	Red	Red	Yellow	Red
Kellys Ford	Green	Green	Green	Yellow	Red	Green
Hogue Tract	Green	Green	Green	Green	Yellow	Green
Remington	Green	Green	Yellow	Green	Red	Yellow
Lakota (Freeman Ford)	Green	Green	Red	Green	Yellow	Red
Springs Road (VA 802)	Green	Green	Red	Green	Green	Red
Warrenton - Lee Highway	Green	Green	Yellow	Green	Yellow	Yellow

Fredericksburg - US 1 Bridge

Google Map Coordinates: 38.320725,-77.471724

Summary Rating

Parking	Green	Spin Fishing	Green
Canoe/Kayak Launch	Yellow	Fly Fishing	Green
Distance to River	Green	Smallmouth Structure	Green
Can Bike to River	Red	Wading Distance	Green
Physical Fitness	Yellow	Pressure	Red
Scenery	Red	Overall	Yellow

The area immediately upstream of the US 1 bridge contains good representative smallmouth bass habitat that provides a dramatic hint of the good water to come. Unfortunately, this part of the river borders the densely populated town of Fredericksburg and receives more than its fair share of pressure. If you are willing to wade away from the shoreline, the pressure dissipates.

Getting to the Stream

North: From I-95, take exit 133A onto US 17 towards Falmouth. Turn right at the intersection with US 1. Go across the bridge and turn right on Hanson Ave followed by another right on Woodford St. At the intersection with Caroline, turn left and park along the road or go right, under the bridge and take another right on Freedom Lane to park in the lot across from the VFW building.

South: From I-95, take exit 130A onto VA 3 towards Fredericksburg. Merge onto US 1 North and follow it to the bridge. Immediately prior to crossing the bridge, turn right on Princess Anne Street followed by a sharp left onto Freedom Lane. Park in the lot on the left or continue down to Caroline Street where you can turn left and park on the side of the road.

If you are a risk taker, there is a small turnoff on Ingleside Drive where it meets the river and starts to run west. To get to that spot, turn west onto W Cambridge Street on the north side of the bridge followed by a right onto VA 1001. Turn left onto Ingleside Drive and look for the small shoulder area. Be alert for any new "No Parking" signs that may have appeared after this book hit the press.

Canoe/Kayak Comment: Old Mill Park, just downstream from the bridge, is a common take-out for canoes and kayaks. There is plenty of parking with a smooth level field bordering the edge of the river and is one of the places that outfitters use to collect their customers. Since the river is flat farther downstream, most paddlers do not go any further.

Environment and Fish

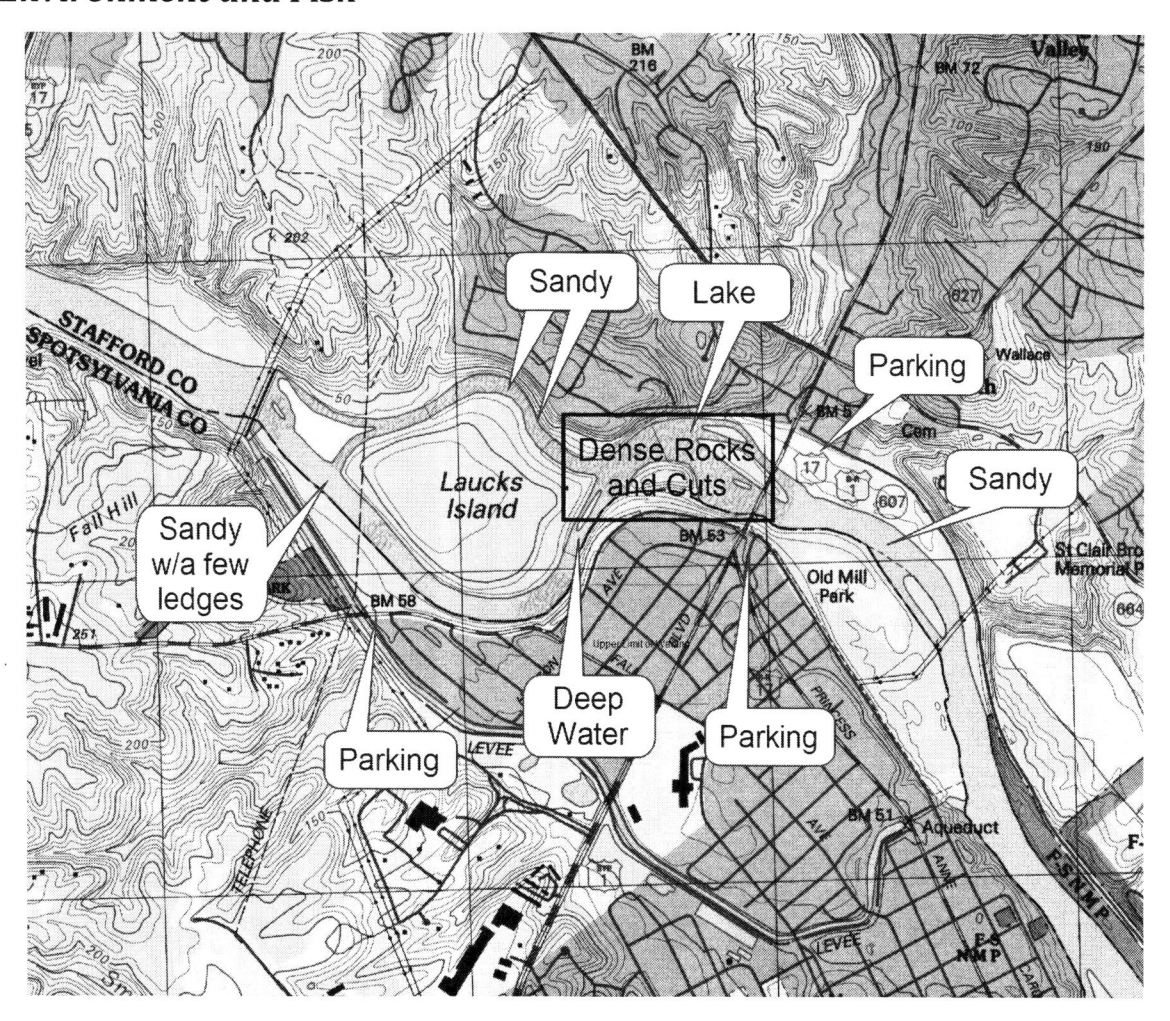

There is only one direction to fish at the US 1 bridge - upstream. The first time you fish here, you may be tempted to pull into Old Mill Park and fish downstream. The river bottom below the US 1 bridge is uniformly sand, generally shallow and barren. While you can park at Old Mill Park, the better choice is to pull off anywhere along Riverside Drive in the vicinity of the bridge or, as described in the directions, in the tight parking lot opposite the Veterans of Foreign Wars building on Freedom Lane. You may also be inclined to park across the river in the parking lot operated by the city of Falmouth. That lot is only open from 8 AM to 7 PM and no trespassing signs speckle the landscape. The town is thorough in enforcing both the hours and the no trespassing restriction – they will lock the gate behind you at 7 PM.

From the VFW parking lot, walk across the street, move to the west edge of the bridge and walk down the beaten path leading to a small sandy beach. As soon as you hit the water and look upstream, your adrenaline will start to pump when you cast your eyes across the channels winding their way through the grass islands; many of which sprout trees and are framed with small whitecaps where the river surges across numerous boulders and ledges.

The area directly under the bridge is a popular swimming location at the height of summer.

If you intend to fish immediately upon entering the water, you have to get to this spot before the swimmers arrive.

Despite the fact that it is a popular hole, you can catch fish in the deep channel on the other side of the first bridge piling.

As you point your rod upstream, the first landmark is a large elongated rock running perpendicular to the stream. Move to it and fish the surrounding deep water. There is a wide run that blows in from the west where the river spills around the major gradient break just upstream. After fishing the perpendicular rock, continue upstream and fish around each of the islands that straddle the middle of the river. The best island is the one with a large, solitary tree growing from it. It marks a key fishing location with good, deep water on either side as a spider web of channels converge on it. The best spot is on the right side.

From there, move south to the deep, wide run that stretches from 38.320316,-77.473264 up to 38.321012,-77.473602. This is directly across from the heavily pressured public beach area on the south bank (38.32065,-77.47320). However, the deep water protects the northern side of the river from pressure. Most people who fish from the shore do not wade across the deep water to reach the middle.

There are two ledges at the start and finish of the run that offer access to the center of the river when the water is low. The key rock ledge is a tall formation, aligned in a north to south direction, at 38.320682,-77.473186. There is a deep pool immediately in front of it that is a constant collection point for sunfish and decent sized bass. Likewise, be sure to work the entrance to the run before you move farther upriver.

From the rocks at 38.32065,-77.47320, the main current splits 50 yards upstream. The flow to the left creates several deeper pools whose boundaries are outlined by many medium sized rocks poking above the river. On the right, the channel is smaller and pushes to the shore, spinning through the middle of the grassy island complex. The strategy to adopt is to stay as far away from the southern bank as possible since it is popular with anglers who are not willing to wade.

After fishing the run in the middle, continue towards the right bank to 38.32215,-77.47396 to explore the large lake where the river pauses before fracturing into many smaller channels downstream. Fish the output before moving upstream. Grass islands frame the lake to the south where they create the boundaries of shallow fast runs while the northern boundary hangs off the steep bank that drops away from Ingleside Drive. As a side comment, the road is not a good access point to the river. While there is a power substation with a broad flat area in front of it, it is clearly marked with "No Parking" signs. There is a solitary, one truck spot at the corner where the road makes the sharp bend to the west at 38.32266,-77.472671, but you risk a ticket if you park there. Go ahead and gut it out and wade up from the bridge.

The deep end of the lake is on the downstream end. You can recognize it from the beach area along the northern shoreline where the locals, who do not have to worry about parking, walk to the river. After you fish the tail of the lake, follow the perimeter outlined by the grass islands and continue to move up the middle of the river. All of your concentration should be on the deep, rocky section at the upper end of the lake that is out of casting range from the shore, but is well within reach from your position in the middle of the river.

The current runs strong down the left edge of the lake. Follow it to the big cluster of logs upstream at 38.32082,-77.47619. At summer levels, you will not have a problem wading along the grass islands to reach the logjam. Walk around the right side of the jam and fish the main channel where it remains deep. In particular, there is a moderate gradient drop between the top of the logjam and the bottom - fish the head of the drop where the river creates a deep pool.

The ledge at 38.32035,-77.47650 marks the farthest you can wade in the center of the river. Upstream is another large, deep lake that is narrow enough to be fished directly from the Park that parallels Riverside Drive. In shad season, this is where people line the banks, shoulder to shoulder, and fish hard. So far, you have hung to the south edge of the main channel. If you want to move across, the best place to do that is to use the sandbar stretching between 38.321545,-77.47494 and 38.32161,-77.47540 at normal water levels. If you do not have a GPS, enter the water at the last large rock that marks the separation between the lake to the north and the start of the fast run next to Mill Island to the south.

Instead of fishing back the way you came, a good option is to swing north and follow the secondary channel leading to the bridge. By and large, it runs from 38.321105,-77.472787 south to 38.320517,-77.471736 and has a trout water feel to it. It is narrow, rocky and deep. In fact, if you find yourself on the northern bank, you have to look carefully to find a place to cross back to the south until you to get closer to the bridge where it shallows out and becomes sandy. One final comment is that the river channel at the far north (Falmouth bank) is not worth fishing. Unlike the terrain to the south, this is where the river lost energy and deposited a considerable amount of silt and sand that rendered the bottom sterile and uninteresting for bass. Stick to the fast water with the rocky bottom.

The initial view from the bottom of the bridge is favorable. Plenty of grass, plenty of rocks and a good flow of water pushing downstream.

A little farther up, the bank of Mill Island begins to appear and it is obvious that the bulk of the current moves along its edge.

Move up and fish around this lone tree. There is a deep hole on the right.

Once done at the tree, move to the left and fish over to Mill Island.

The main channel runs next to Mill Island. You are in a good position fishing it from the center of the river since it is too deep to wade across from the shore. Be sure to hit both sides of the set of rapids at the top.

Above the rapids, another spectacular vista of scattered grass islands, deep holes and rocks awaits (shown at 48 cfs).

Fish over to the big lake on the right near the northern shore. This is the view looking upriver...

... and this is the view looking downriver.

Fish up the deep channel that leads to the tangled stack of logs - there are numerous good channels with high rock ridges facilitating wading.

On the other side of the logs, the deep water begins - leading to the bend where the river turns north (below the Virginia Outdoor Center).

On the way back, move down the northern channel leading to the bridge.

The northern channel has a trout water feel to it. The depth and velocity of the current keeps you on the shore.

Laucks Island

If you are obsessive about fishing everything, and worked up to the logjam and crossed the river, you will notice the wide channel that joins the river on the north side of Laucks Island. To give the bottom line up front, do not waste energy fishing around the northern perimeter. The flow is not strong and disintegrates into a series of small, shallow runs where it joins the main river. At the junction, there is a large pool surrounded by several big boulders that sometimes holds bass. Once you fish that spot and raise your eyes to the north, notice the additional pools in the distance separated by well-defined rapids that compress the channel and create a few places of interest.

At 38.32106,-77.47792, there is a large lake that is worth fishing ...only if you are already there. It is too deep to wade up the middle, forcing you to pick a shoreline. Both are reasonably open with the right bank offering the easiest path forward. The bottom, since this is a side water, is mostly sand, but there are enough boulders to provide minimal holding structure for smallmouth. The farther you move away from the main river, the fewer the smallmouth.

Once beyond the first major lake, the river fractures as it runs around a dense field of large boulders. There are small shallow runs that segment the boulder field, emerging from a lake created by a dam formed by a large rock running perpendicular to the riverbed at 38.322586,-77.479867.

If you get this far, this is where you should stop and turn back. While there is a large lake that curves around the bend to your front, the bottom is totally sandy with no compelling current to make it an interesting place for anything but sunfish. If you persist and walk to the upper end of the lake, the river shallows out even further and becomes a sad trickle that is only inches deep. If you have not turned around yet, this is where you should really give up and head back to more pleasant water.

The entry to the channel that runs around the north side of the island is promising. You can pick up a fish or two right here.

On the other side of the rocks, this broad lake opens up. It is not wadeable, but you can move around the edges.

At the top, there is a nice set of narrow channels that compresses the water.

Beyond that, it is a stagnant lake - no water volume to speak of at 48 cfs.

Riverside Drive

The next spot to fish is the area along Riverside Drive. Unlike the tough terrain you had to stagger through immediately upstream of the bridge, this section is framed by easy, rolling parkland on the southern shore. When the water levels are right, you can fish all the way up to the Friends of the Rappahannock/Virginia Outdoor Center just below the site of the old Embry Dam that was removed in 2004. One place you cannot wade is in the deep section that extends from the confluence at Laucks Island to where the riffle occurs at the junction of Wellford Street with Riverside Drive. There is easy access to the deep area from the shore and I recommend using spinning gear because there is no room for a fly rod backcast. At 38.318032,-77.478038, walk out on some of the rock ledges to fish the fast current downstream of the ledge that extends at a 45° angle across the river. From here to the bend, access is limited to the shallow shelf that runs along the shoreline. The river has decent depth and you will eventually be closed out in the vicinity of 38.316696,-77.479025 where the river begins to turn around the corner formed by the lower perimeter of Laucks Island.

Starting at 38.316721,-77.48004, there are seven lines of rocks that stretch across the river. These form the only interesting structure that has the potential to hold fish between the corner and the site where the Embry Dam used to sit. You have to stay in the river beyond the fourth set of ledges because the property on the left bank belongs to the Friends of the Rappahannock/Virginia Outdoor Center. If you are a member of their organization, you can use that property without restriction. Given the better water immediately upstream in the vicinity of the I-95 bridge, it is not worth fishing this particular section even though it is accessible. The key issue that makes this a marginal location is that when the Embry Dam was removed, all of the accumulated silt washed downstream. It will take many years of Spring floods to clean out the sand and improve the habitat for fish.

If you decide to proceed, the ledges are located at:

- 38.316721,-77.48004
- 38.316763,-77.481499
- 38.316797,-77.482186
- 38.317033,-77.48284
- 38.317394,-77.48342
- 38.317756,-77.483978
- 38.318514,-77.484911

Move directly to the ledges and do not bother to fish the dead zones between them.

From the middle of Riverside Drive, the view into the bend is pleasing and encouraging at 48 cfs. At summer lows, it is easy to wade.	Do not neglect the area adjacent to the Park. You can wade from the line of rapids at the top right corner.

Upstream of the bend, the seven ledges are the only fishable structure; the rest is sand.

A closer view of the seven ledges - barely visible above the water at 49 cfs.

Bottom Line

Even though this area is heavily pressured, most is from the shore. If you are willing to wade and negotiate the boulder field, you can find plenty of good pools that hold decent fish.

Fredericksburg - I-95 Bridge

Google Map Coordinates: 38.326373,-77.501035

Summary Rating

Parking	**Green**	Spin Fishing	**Green**
Canoe/Kayak Launch	**Red**	Fly Fishing	**Green**
Distance to River	**Red**	Smallmouth Structure	**Green**
Can Bike to River	**Green**	Wading Distance	**Green**
Physical Fitness	**Yellow**	Pressure	**Green**
Scenery	**Green**	Overall	**Green**

The I-95 bridge is one of the treasures of the Rappahannock. You have probably driven across the bridge 1,000 times and wondered about the water below. I'm here to tell you that this is an excellent place protected by a mile walk on an easy trail that filters out all of the pressure. Most people simply do not want to walk anywhere.

Getting to the Stream

North: From I-95, take exit 133A onto US 17 towards Falmouth. Turn right at the intersection with US 1. Go across the bridge and turn right on Hanson Ave followed by another right on Woodford St. At the intersection with Caroline, turn left and follow Caroline to the Friends of the Rappahannock property next to the river. Immediately after passing the Friends property, pull into the small parking area on the left side of the street (38.316508,-77.485821).

South: From I-95, take exit 130A onto VA 3 towards Fredericksburg. Merge onto US 1 North and follow it to the bridge. Immediately prior to crossing the bridge, turn right on Princess Anne Street followed by a sharp left onto Freedom Lane. Continue to Caroline Street and make a left to follow Caroline to the Friends of the Rappahannock property next to the river. Immediately after passing Friends property, pull into the small parking area on the left side of the street (38.316508,-77.485821).

To reach the water, go across the street, through the gate and follow the road next to the canal to the river (38.321155,-77.489727).

Canoe/Kayak Comment: Unless you are a member of the Friends of the Rappahannock, you cannot use their property to launch or extract a canoe near the old Embry Dam. You can take-out immediately prior to reaching their property, but that results in a half mile walk to the public parking along the canal. A better place to put-in or take-out is a little farther downstream where the river runs next to the road. There is a small strip of public park that spans the gap and provides access. You will have to haul your boat up a one to two foot bank to reach the grassy shoreline.

Environment and Fish

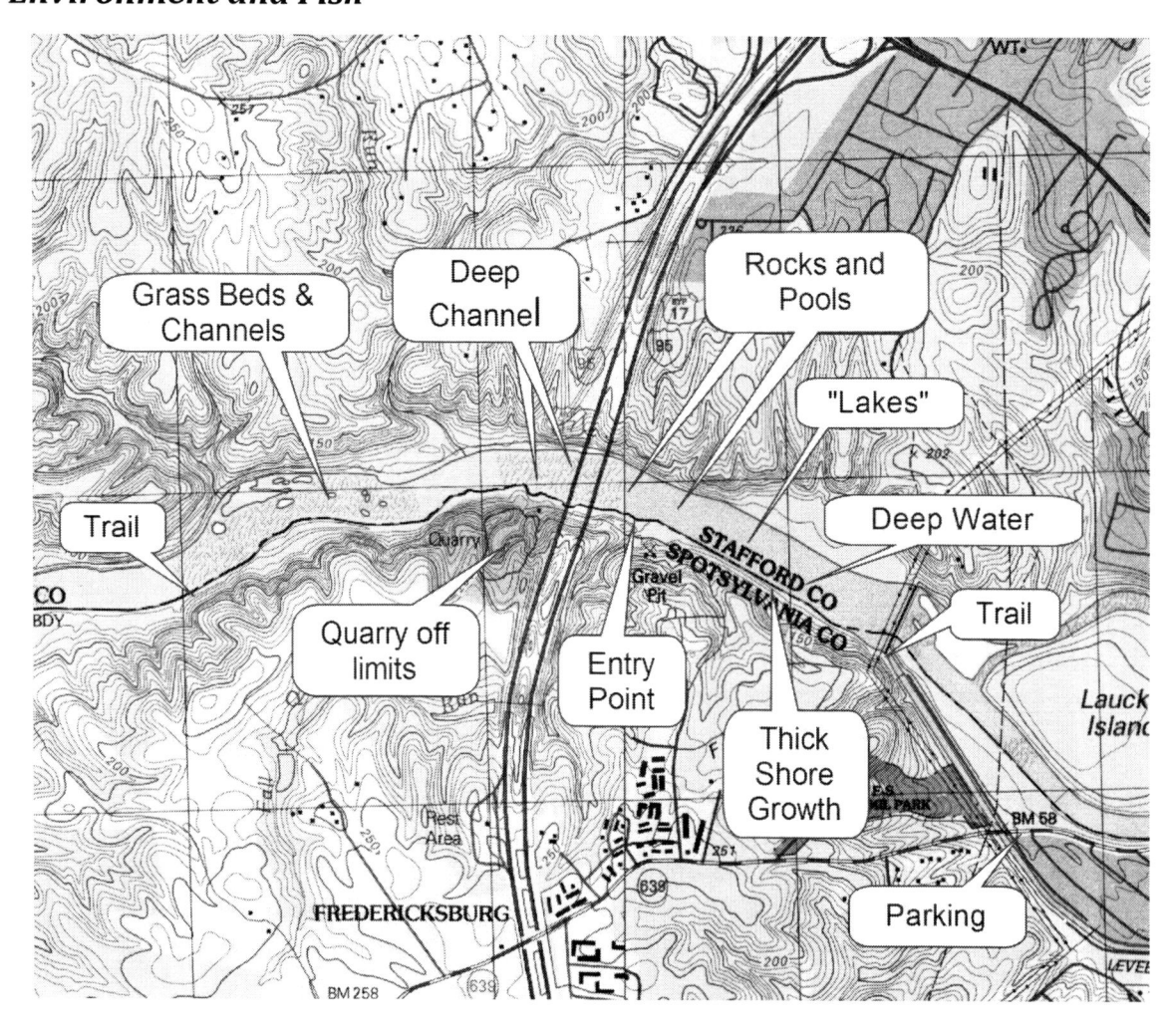

Once on the river at 38.320997,-77.489567, you are at the site of the old Embry Dam. The monument that marks the destruction is a few feet away from the fence line that has placards with historical information. The property on the right is private and owned by the Friends of the Rappahannock. If you join their organization, you can use their property to access the river. For the next mile downstream, the silt that dumped out of Embry Dam coats the bottom of the river. Granted, while there are a few ledges providing holding structure for fish, moving downstream is normally a waste of time. From where you stand, you have three choices:

- Begin fishing upstream right away
- Walk to the bridge and fish the quarter mile on each side of the bridge
- Walk upstream as far you can go and fish back to the bridge

Upstream to the Bridge

If you elect the first choice, you are about to fish the worst part of the I-95 section. Since the Embry Dam sat here for many years, silt accumulated on the upstream side. Luckily, much of the silt has moved downstream, but the next 800 feet upstream still holds plenty of mud. Enter at the monument. Access to the river from the trail that runs along the southern bank is extremely limited, if not impossible. The trail is just far enough away from the river to allow a dense thicket of poison ivy and pricker bushes to grow without restriction. All the vines have intertwined with small saplings and bushes to create an impenetrable fence. Therefore, once you are in the river fishing upstream, you are condemned to stay there until exiting at the small parking area at 38.324819,-77.497775.

If you choose to fish upstream, wade to the sandbar approximately 3/4 of the way across the river at 38.323144,-77.491166. Since it is a little higher, the mud is minimized and you can fish the sandy channel between it and the southern shore without sinking to your knees. Once you realize there is not much action, continue west to the tip of the island and the first ridgeline that stretches across the river at 38.323497,-77.492622. Thick sand and mud encases the rocks, but, just upstream, the river begins to shift and offer a more smallmouth friendly, rocky bottom. Push through the mud to the broad set of ledges that stretch entirely across the river at 38.323891,-77.493394. This is the first good fishing in the upstream slog. Fish between the rocks and in the many cuts with an intense focus on the downstream side. Do not bother with the northern half of the ridge, the southern section is best since it features better bottom structure as well as deeper water.

Unfortunately, the river presents another set of lemons just upstream of the ridgelines - one more muddy lake. The lake is about 400 feet with mud coating both banks. In fact, you may find yourself closed out depending on how far you sink into the mud. If that happens, your only choice is to hack through the brush on the southern shoreline or beat back to the monument. Once at the next ridgeline upstream (38.324758,-77.495298), you are finally into the good water that extends 1,200 feet up to the bridge.

This is the upper end where the river starts the run to the bridge and turns into rocks with good ledges.

The good water is upriver from this rock. Picture taken at 151 cfs.

I-95 Bridge

Hopefully, you followed my advice and did not enter the water at the Embry Dam. Instead, walk up the beaten trail that stretches along the southern boundary of the river. You will encounter a sign marking the start of private property. As this book goes to press, the public is permitted access through the property on the trail. This is confirmed by the many signs that caution about wearing blaze orange during hunting season. A point of warning about the trail is that every few years, the landowner has to actually "post" the property for a short period of time to keep from establishing a prescriptive easement that would relinquish their rights to control access. Hopefully, if the current landowner sells the property, the next landowner maintains the open attitude towards the public. If this is ever closed to the public, I'll update the book with an alternative route, if one exists, to get to the bridge area based on the property situation at that time.

If you have a bike, this is the perfect place to use it. The trail actually extends three miles along the river from the Friends of the Rappahannock. Once past the bad section that was impacted by the Embry Dam, everything is great. Bike or hike up the trail until reaching the parking lot at 38.324785,-77.497872. Sadly, there is no public access to that lot with a vehicle. If there was, it would really make it easy. Enter the water using the trail that extends from the parking lot to the river. Everything in front of you is good! Looking downstream, there are tall rocks creating a barrier that backs up deep pools on the upstream side. Climb through the large boulders to teeter out on the ledges looking for the few narrow gaps where the river forces its way through to continue downstream. Each is an ideal holding place for fish.

Once you finish with the deep pool upstream of the major rock formation at 38.325345,-77.497012, climb down onto the sandbar that runs parallel to the direction of flow. The deep section is on the northern side; wade out to attack the holes near the ledges that run perpendicular to the sandbar.

Between the parking lot and the I-95 bridge itself, the river constructs a veritable maze of channels with deep drop-offs with the major one being immediately upstream -- approximately 150 feet -- from the entry point at 38.325962,-77.498745. It will take you a long time to work around the edges of this pool, but it will be worth it. Move back to the southern shore to avoid the silt on the north and continue to wade towards the bridge following the main flow of the current. From the lower boundary of the pool, aim toward the spot where the I-95 bridge crosses the northern shoreline (38.327133,-77.500843). While the other sections are good, the deeper channels - and the most fish - are along that general line.

The water under the bridge is diverse. The closer to the southern bank you get, the shallower it becomes. However, be attentive to the few deep sections. If short on time, move directly to the northern bank and follow the main channel of the river that runs at a 45° angle back towards the southern bank. You cannot miss the channel since it is cradled by a large island that lurches out of the river between 38.326847,-77.502414 and 38.326433,-77.503717. Continue to follow the channel into a lazy S-curve, swinging back to the north approximately 200 feet upstream to dodge around a complex of rocks that extends into the river at 38.326404,-77.506759. It is not worth moving all the way to the northern bank since the water shallows out and becomes sandy on that side. Instead, follow the channel around the northern perimeter of the rocks as it loops back to the join the shore at 38.325402,-77.508803.

There are plenty of rocks that define numerous gradient breaks – all back up good pools.

The largest pool is at the entry point. Use the rocks on the far right to fish the lower perimeter.

This is the start of the best channel just north of the bridge at 151 cfs. It runs around the corner into the next picture.

This is the deep channel that runs along the rocky protrusion from the southern bank.

I-95 Bridge Upstream

The first batch of rapids stretches across the river with the major complex being 800 feet upstream at 38.325492,-77.513675. Move to the middle of the river, and cover the deep section. You may find it difficult to wade in some areas and that will force you towards the northern bank.

The good rocks extend 1,200 feet -- all the way upstream to 38.323521,-77.517488. The river returns to sand for the next 300 feet and then enters a final rocky section with numerous perpendicular ledges extending across the river starting at 38.323353,-77.519225 and continuing upstream for an additional 800 feet. Beyond that point, the river deepens and loses the favorable smallmouth structure with only random pockets of the rocks. The next decent fishable area is within 3,000 feet of the good water downstream from Motts Run (38.321488,-77.526479). It is a much shorter walk to reach that area starting from Motts rather than from the trail leading up from the Friends of the Rappahannock.

You have three distinct choices near the bridge and which you pick depends on how far you are willing to walk or bike. The trail along the river is flat and easy to negotiate. There are no obstacles to using a bike and that is the best choice to move quickly to the great water. My personal preference is to start at 38.324106,-77.514793 and fish all the way back to the upper (restricted) parking lot. I generally skip the section that was impacted by the old Embry Dam. If you want to start at the same spot, follow the trail until you see a bench off to the right where the trail rejoins the river. Wade out and have at it. You can spend an hour fishing the good cuts within 300 feet of the bench.

Look for this bench and enter the river here.

Fish up or downstream? Both are good. This is the view upstream.

Downstream from the entry point reveals a broad river heavily populated with grass beds, rocks and the associated channels.

Every wide spot holds decent sized fish even at 93 cfs.

I-95 Bridge 43

Be prepared to pick up a couple of these guys - the 20 inchers live here. As always, caught and released - please do the same.

The good water extends all the way down to the I-95 bridge in the distance.

The Quarry

I mention the quarry because you might be tempted to fish it. Do not. It is off limits for fishing and the signs at the access point provide plenty of warning in English and Spanish. Besides, local law enforcement agencies use the quarry to do scuba and rescue training. It would be pretty embarrassing to be caught fishing by a couple of truckloads of police.

Besides, if you walk up to the edge, you will quickly conclude that it is just not fishable. There is a twenty yard section next to the road/trail that overlooks deep water, but beyond the narrow edge, the stark walls of the quarry limit access. Blow it off and move up the trail to the better water on the river.

The quarry is deep with abrupt sides that justify the prohibition against fishing.

Bottom Line

The I-95 bridge is one of the top five places on the Rappahannock to fish. The key attraction is its close proximity to the major highway system. You can zip down I-95 and find yourself in spectacular water with a very short one mile walk from the parking area. Many of the other good locations require either a longer drive on back roads or a longer walk, beating through the undergrowth and fighting off ticks.

Motts Run

Google Map Coordinates: 38.308932,-77.530518

Summary Rating

Parking	**Red**	Spin Fishing	**Green**
Canoe/Kayak Launch	**Green**	Fly Fishing	**Green**
Distance to River	**Green**	Smallmouth Structure	**Green**
Can Bike to River	**Red**	Wading Distance	**Green**
Physical Fitness	**Yellow**	Pressure	**Red**
Scenery	**Green**	Overall	**Yellow**

If you only fish along River Road, you will be deeply disappointed. Between the pull-off at the bend and the Clore Brothers Outfitters upstream, the river is hammered, intensely pressured and very crowded on weekends. But, if you are willing to walk 2,000 feet downstream, you will be by yourself in another great place to fish.

Getting to the Stream

From I-95, take exit 130-B west, continue on VA 3 (Plank Road) approximately 0.5 mile; turn right on VA 639 (Bragg Road) and go about one mile to River Road. Turn left on VA 618 (River Road), follow it down the hill (38.308932,-77.530518). There is a small turnoff where the road begins to parallel the river.

Canoe/Kayak Comment: This is a popular put-in location for those who do not want to spend the extra time paddling downriver from the VDGIF public launch near the Clore Brothers Outfitters. The picture shows the short walk to the river.

It does not make sense to take-out here since it is only flat water between Clore Brothers and this access point. You may as well use the public launch next to their facility. This is a good place to put-in for the short, quick run down to the US 1 bridge.

Environment and Fish

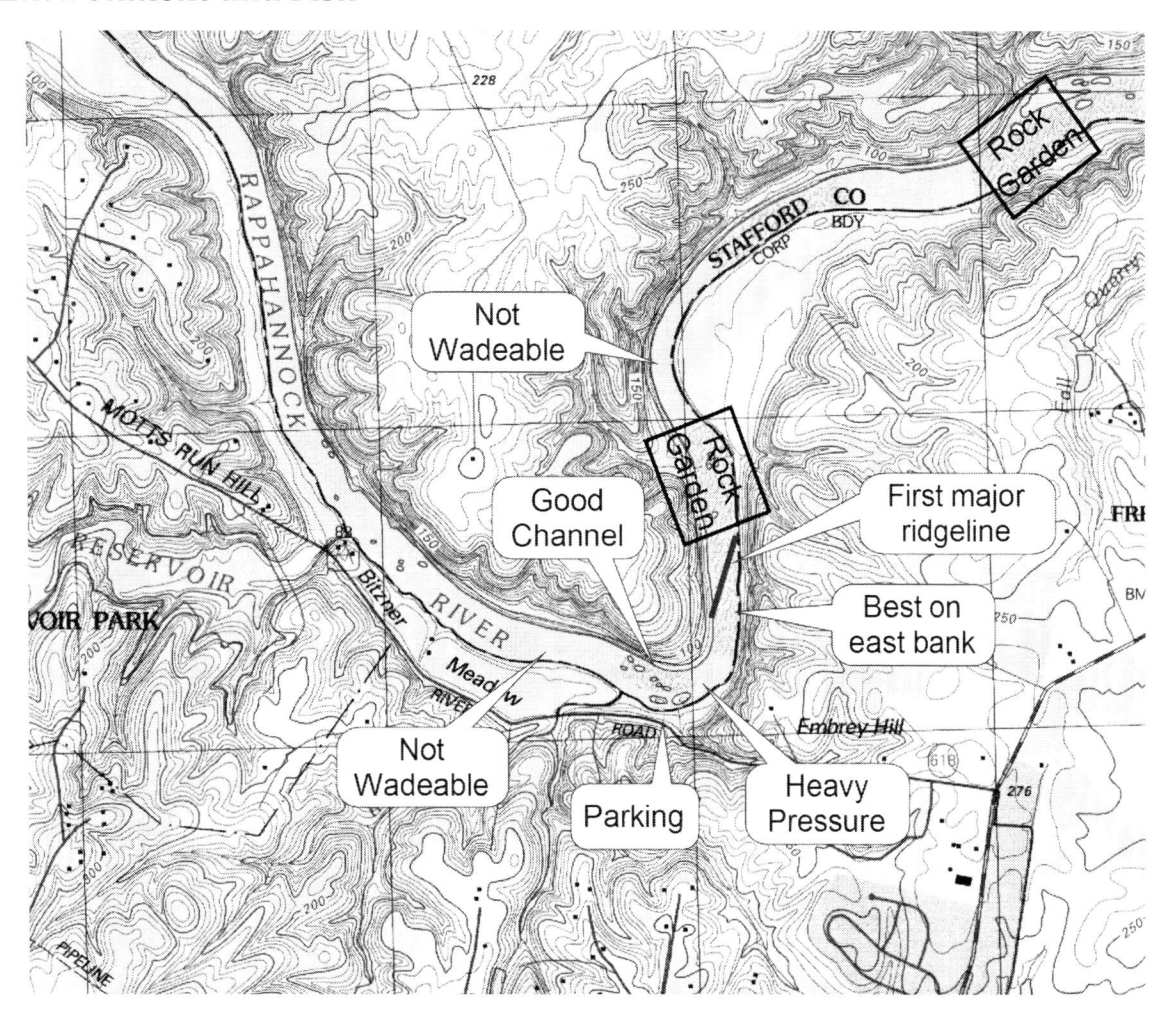

Map of Motts Run area with labels: Rock Garden, Not Wadeable, Good Channel, First major ridgeline, Best on east bank, Not Wadeable, Parking, Heavy Pressure, Rock Garden.

If you talk to most anglers, they will instantly caution that Motts Run is a poor choice. The bad "rapp" (sorry... I had to insert that pun at least once in this book) comes from the intense fishing pressure. What many fail to realize is that an investment of a little sweat and energy to move downstream will put you on excellent water that is infested with bass. If you only walk upstream, you will share the common opinion and make a personal resolution never to return.

Upstream

If you intend to fish upstream from Motts Run, you have two choices at the end of the short path leading to the river. Neither will put you on good water and that makes the discussion short.

The first choice is to fish up the left bank with the alternative being to walk directly across to fish the channel downstream of the large rocks to the left front. The left bank features a wide, shallow shelf that eventually closes out in the broad lake that extends up to the Clore Brothers Outfitters a mile upriver (38.30926,-77.53068).

If you chose the alternative and move to the right bank, you will be closed out by the lake at approximately the same place (38.31030,-77.53034). Once there, slide downstream to fish the four to five foot deep hole in back of the large logjam. It is actually pretty good if you fish it early in the season before the crowds arrive. Downstream of the logjam, there are a series of small runs paralleling the left bank. Since all terminate in the lake at the bend on the left edge of the river, they are heavily fished by people who do not realize the treasure trove that sits a mere half mile downstream from the parking area. The pictures tell the story in terms of the human activity within the hundred yard circle that surrounds the parking area. Beyond the pressure, many of the runs are too shallow to hold fish since the river widens as it runs through the complex maze of grass beds that tuck up next to the parking area.

The view up the left bank at 176 cfs. Ignore the left bank - go to the right.

The log complex at the right along the northern bank is the best place to start.

48   Motts Run

Above this spot, the river turns into an unwadeable lake.

The good channel runs down the north bank.

This is the good spot on the other side of the logjam on the north side of the river at 182 cfs.

There is a hole immediately in front of this set of rocks at the bend on the north side.

Heavy, heavy pressure. Kayakers, canoeists and anglers all compete for space within feet of the parking area.

If this was not so pressured, it would be a great place. This is the view upstream from the bend.

Downstream

Walk down the wide dirt path to the river's edge. To the front is a wide expanse of water featuring grass beds with narrow, shallow runs leading into the bend to the northeast. Skip the shallow section immediately in front of the parking area despite the fact that it is peppered with rocks and tempting channels . Walk directly over the long sandbar (38.309709,-77.526865) leading to the bend and fish the deep section where the river turns left. Leverage the rock ridge that parallels the deep section to move to the right bank. That bank has the majority of rock structure and, from it, you can launch attacks towards the deeper water in the center. There are numerous holes that range up to four feet deep interspersed with rocks on the right bank. Therefore, do not blunder ahead - fish carefully downstream.

The key initial feature between the bend and the first rock complex is a series of narrow ridges that run parallel with the flow and are most obvious at 38.311454,-77.526271. Each creates a channel that holds deep water, usually on the western side. To the extent you can wade out into the center, fish each channel in turn. Shift to the right bank where there is a large boulder approximately 50 yards downstream of the start of the very visible, major rock formation that extends from 38.3117,-77.526658 to 38.313506,-77.526106. Starting at the boulder, there are deep holes scattered along the shore that are perfect for a surface lure. Travel downriver, following the main current that moves along the right bank. If there are kayakers going downriver, watch the way they go and that will tell you where the deep channel is. At 38.31204,-77.52592, just after the large rock on the right, start to move to the center of the river. Cautiously approach the first set of rocks because there is a nice hole on the right. Continue toward it on a squared off rock ridge. Have a lure tied on that will run six to seven feet deep as you approach.

Wade across the river to the base of the elevated line of rocks. Fish the deep cut to the front and then walk around to climb up on the ridgeline. When the water is clear, that perch provides a good view of the terrain. To the right there are channels, framed by the ridges, with extremely deep water on the right that shallows up a touch where the flow collides with the ridge. On the left, there are scattered pools surrounded by rocks and vegetation. All is good. Focus on the areas that have grass and rocks and ignore the sandy spots. There is a deep section on the right. When done, continue to use the rock ridge to move downriver. At 38.31295,-77.52631, the river takes a cut between the rock ridge that marks the place where you must make a decision to go left or right. Before you do either, be sure you fish the six foot deep hole on the downstream right side of the gap in the ridgeline.

On the left, there are scattered pools with sandy bottoms outlined by boulders and a minimum of grass. You may want to wander over to the left bank to fish up against the grass beds in the pools that lie in that direction. Alternatively, proceed along the ridgelines, keeping the center of the river to the left, fishing the good spots as you go. 38.31321,-77.52617 is the other major break between the ridge and the river. Like 38.31295,-77.52631, it features a deep hole on the downstream side. At this point, turn right and hit the bank if the shade is on the water. Coming up on the left are a series of deep holes - throw to the middle. Just up the ridgeline from 38.31321,-77.52617, there is a small peninsula that sticks out into the center of the river. Use it to gain access to the deep hole. There are several places you can move into the center of the river from the peninsula. Move left around the shallow shelf or get up on the tall rock next to it to survey the scene.

To the front, there is another high rock ridge that runs parallel with the river. Hop on it to wade out to hit the center lake, which is the best part in this section. Go deep and spend a decent amount of time fishing everything. Continue moving up the right bank. Being a creature of habit, that is the way I always go because I want to fish the four foot deep water that hugs the bank underneath trees featuring plenty of fallen logs. There may be a way across the river earlier, but I go all the way up to where the next set of angled ridges join the river. Once there, enjoy the wonderful rock garden that stretches all the way to the bend. Fish the terminus of every cut. There are no particular landmarks here, you will see it when you arrive. The rock garden starts at 38.31539,-77.52618 and is 0.83 miles from the parking area.

38.31551,-77.52698 is the lake in the center of the rock garden. Most of the river funnels through this feature, pushing food to the waiting fish. When approaching the bottom of the rock garden, do not blunder forward. There are several four foot deep areas at the end of runs. Patiently fish to the grass island and then make up your mind whether you want to go any farther. Downstream, the river turns into another lake as it runs around the bend and quickly becomes too deep to wade. The grass island at 38.31720,-77.52827 is a little over one mile from the parking lot. It marks the end of the rock garden and your downstream journey. Do not hurry through any section other than the first quarter mile. Since it is close to the parking lot, it experiences the most pressure and the bottom is horribly sandy.

Assuming you walked downstream on the right bank, you need to fish back on the left (river left). In particular, the area near that bank is initially grassy and three to four feet deep, with a good spot around a tangle of fallen logs and brush at 38.31456,-77.52733. The entire area around the logs is another calm lake. Fish the lake, concentrating on the fast current seams. After you fish the logjam, the bank shallows out and becomes uninteresting as you plod up the shallow cuts running between the numerous grass beds. The only reason to return on this side is that you do not have to cross the river again. Also, by staying on the west bank, you get to fish the lake areas from the opposite direction.

Upstream of the rock garden, the bank is uniformly shallow and unproductive up to the last ridge near the bend. In particular, 38.31221,-77.52697 represents an area you should skip. Although the bottom is rock, it is flat rock with no structure to hold fish. Walk through quickly.

If you do not have much time when you come to Motts Run, walk directly across from the parking area to 38.30972,-77.52797 where there is a small lake area with a good run that dumps into the bend. While you may not catch anything large, the lake has plenty of sunfish and, at times, a few smallmouth. If you want to go directly to the rock garden, there is no need to walk down the right bank. While the fishing is better on that side, it is harder to walk over as a result of all of the awkwardly positioned boulders. It is much easier to cross directly over to the left (west) bank and walk down the shallow shelf to the rock garden. By doing that, you cut off 0.3 miles from the walk and get to the best fishing quickly.

Your initial step into the river shows nice scenery down to the bend.

This is the first ridge of rocks and marks the lower boundary of the rock garden at 182 cfs.

The view on the other side of the first ridge is encouraging and the fishing is good.

The initial part of the rock garden features plenty of grass islands that shelter good pools.

This is the main lake. Work around the edges while fishing the main current seam that runs through the middle.

This is the heart of the rock garden at 176 cfs.

This small grass island marks the end of wadeable water.

Upstream from the turnaround point reveals a labyrinth of rocks and channels to fish.

Bottom Line

If you are not willing to walk downstream from Motts Run, do not bother with this section. However, there is a "pot of gold" for those willing to beat directly down the western bank to the dense ridge and grass area that is about 2,500 feet away from the parking.

Motts Run Reservoir

Google Map Coordinates: 38.315552,-77.55568

Summary Rating

Parking	**Green**	Spin Fishing	**Green**
Canoe/Kayak Launch	**Green**	Fly Fishing	**Green**
Distance to River	**Green**	Smallmouth Structure	**Red**
Can Bike to River	**Red**	Wading Distance	**Red**
Physical Fitness	**Green**	Pressure	**Yellow**
Scenery	**Green**	Overall	**Yellow**

If you need a largemouth bass fishing fix, this 160 acre lake is the place to go since it is close to the river. It has good public facilities - although you will pay a day use fee to take advantage of them.

Getting to the Lake

Option 1: From I-95, take exit 130-B west, continue on VA 3 (Plank Road) approximately 0.5 mile, turn right on VA 639 (Bragg Road) and go about one mile to River Road. Turn left on VA 618 (River Road), follow it down the hill to the river (38.308932,-77.530518). Continue along the road until you see the sign for the Reservoir. Turn left and follow the road to the parking area.

Canoe/Kayak Comment: There is an improved boat launch at the Reservoir. You have to pay a day use fee.

Environment and Fish

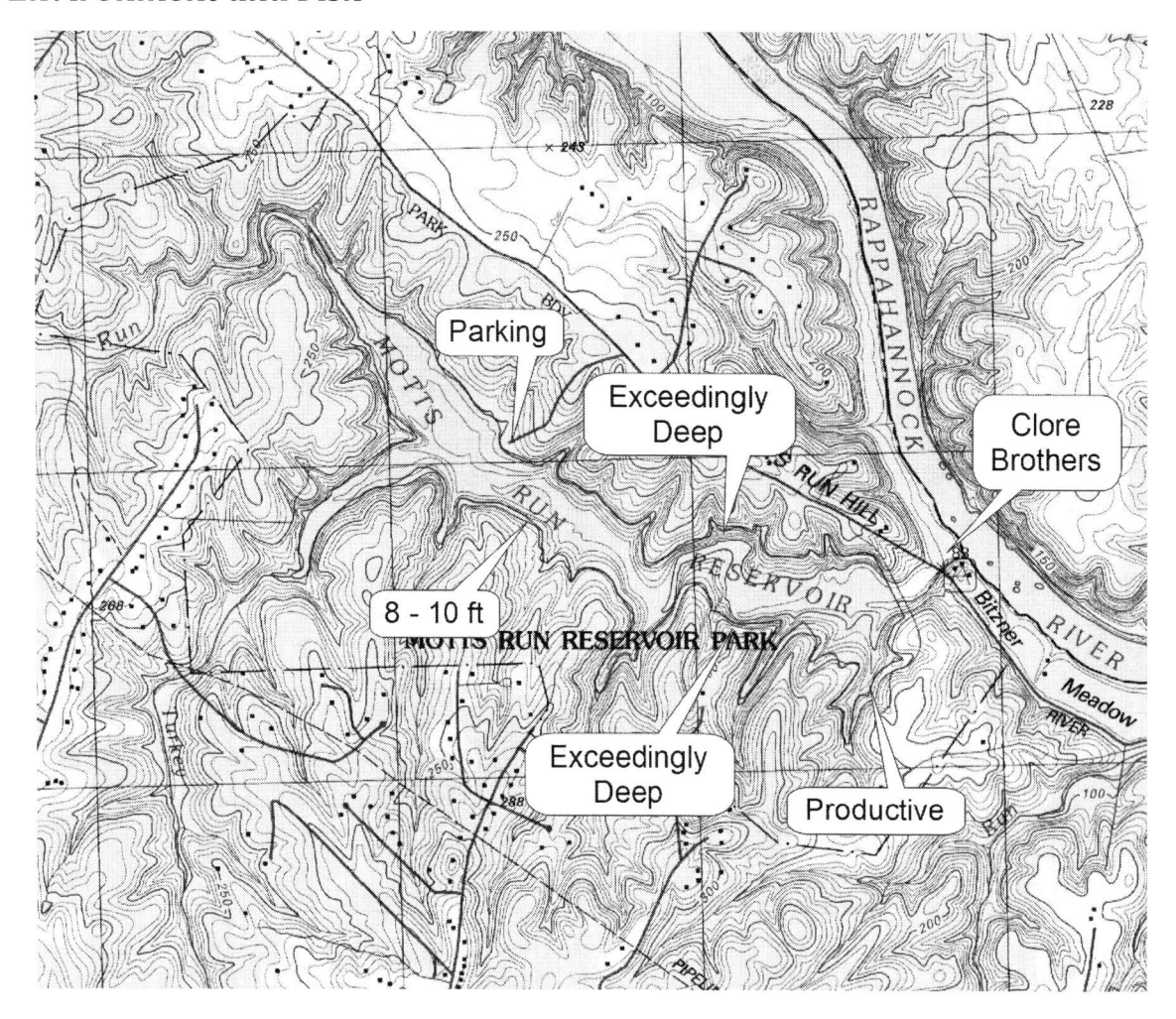

The lake is open between April and October with good facilities for families including a concession stand, toilets and picnic tables. There are fishing piers with fish attractors. While it is not wadeable and you have to pay a fee to use it, Motts is a nice lake that is fishable from the shoreline in the immediate area of the concession stand.

If you drop a canoe or kayak in the water, the first thing to notice is that there is a lack of shoreline structure. While there is vegetation growing next to the shore, there are no blowdowns or other fish attractors beyond the piers. In fact, the VDIGF website states that the lake was scraped clean of structure when it was formed - so it is slick as a greased skillet - nothing there except whatever hidden underwater brush piles/beaver dens were created after the lake was filled.

This is a DEEP lake! You can sit 10 feet from the shore and be in 40 feet of water on the northern shore - something else that makes it a real challenge to fish. The few times I fished it, my fishfinder rarely picked up any fish swimming around in the deep water - leading me to believe that they hole up in the weeds along the side of the lake. Therefore, I recommend you adopt the technique of working down the shoreline with the best approach on a breezy day being to back your kayak into the weed bed and then cast up and down the shore. The other approach is to stick with the southern shore where the depth ranges between eight and ten feet, allowing you to fish normally.

The VDGIF site claims that the lake gets light fishing pressure. I have never experienced a solitary day fishing here. Most summer weekends see plenty of other anglers in pursuit of the largemouth bass, catfish, white perch and northern pike that live in the lake. The concession stand rents boats outfitted with an electric motor, and those craft are well used.

Grass beds with good points are always productive.

View back up towards the boat launch from the southern shore.

Bottom Line

If you need to catch a largemouth and do not mind paying the fee, Motts Reservoir is decent - but I would rather hit the river.

Clore Brothers

Google Map Coordinates: 38.31373,-77.541128

Summary Rating

Parking	Green	Spin Fishing	Green
Canoe/Kayak Launch	Green	Fly Fishing	Green
Distance to River	Green	Smallmouth Structure	Yellow
Can Bike to River	Red	Wading Distance	Green
Physical Fitness	Green	Pressure	Red
Scenery	Yellow	Overall	Yellow

Do not be put off by all of the vehicles in the broad parking lot that defines the northern boundary of the Clore Brothers Outfitters operation. Many belong to kayakers and canoeists who will be dead-tired and happy after a long, hot day of paddling. While this area sees a significant amount of fishing pressure, many anglers do not venture far enough away from the launch to enjoy the best it can offer. If you walk a little, you can have a great day.

Getting to the Stream

From I-95, take exit 130-B west, continue on VA 3 (Plank Road) approximately 0.5 mile, turn right on VA 639 (Bragg Road) and go about one mile to River Road. Turn left on VA 618 (River Road), follow it down the hill to the river (38.308932,-77.530518). Continue west on River Road until you pass the Clore Brothers Outfitters. Make a right turn into the VDGIF launch area (38.31373,-77.541128) after you pass the entrance to the Clore facility.

Canoe/Kayak Comment: One of the best put-in and take-out points on the river is located adjacent to the Clore Brothers facility. It has wooden stairs with a canoe slide that makes the insertion or extraction of a boat relatively easy. The broad parking area holds plenty of vehicles.

Environment and Fish

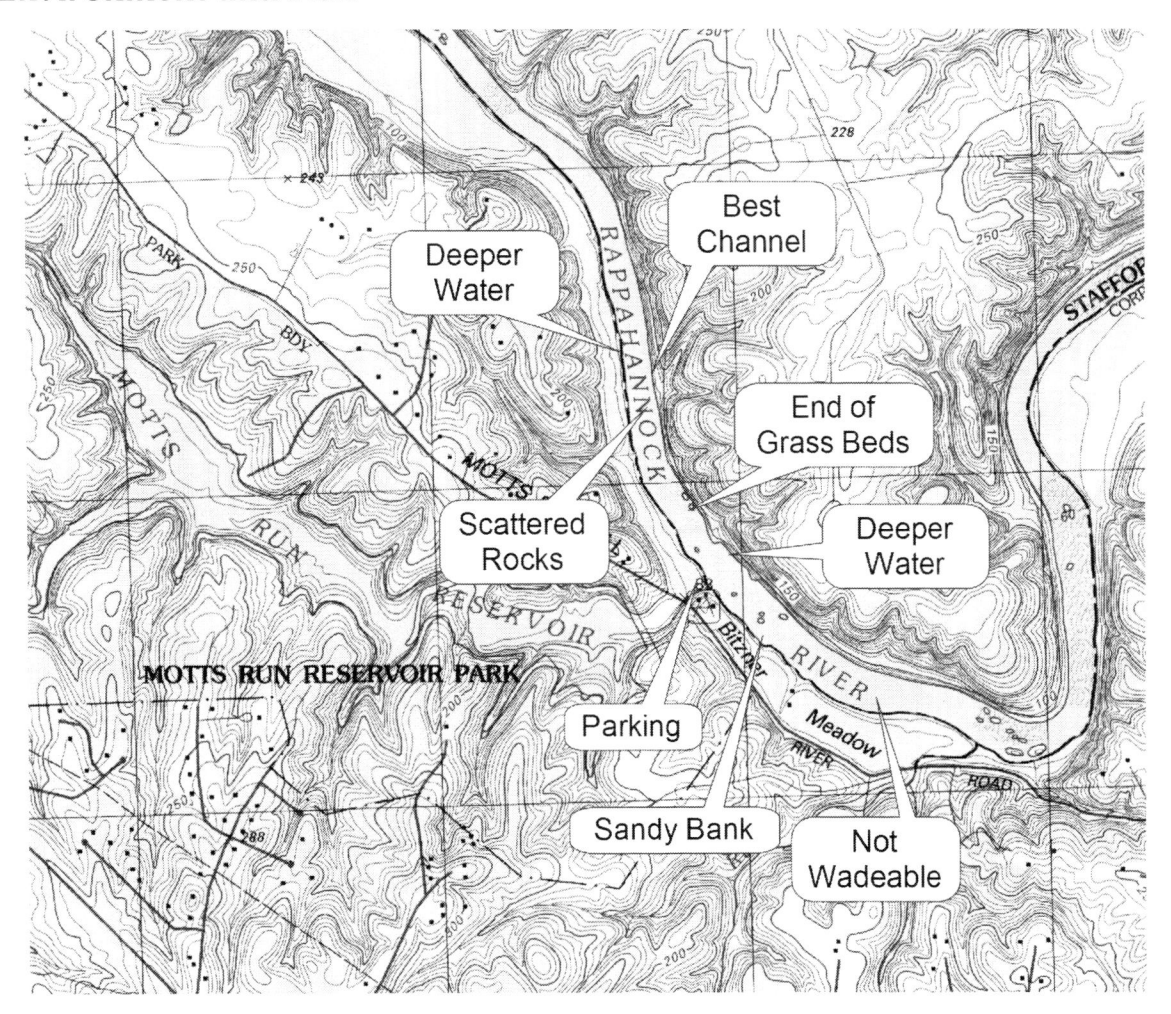

[Topographic map showing a section of the Rappahannock River near Motts Run Reservoir Park, with labels: Deeper Water, Best Channel, End of Grass Beds, Scattered Rocks, Deeper Water, Parking, Sandy Bank, Not Wadeable]

Upstream

As you look at the exhausted, yet satisfied, expressions on the faces of the kayakers and canoeists staggering up the stairs that parallel the canoe slide, you might assume that this section is lightly pressured. After all, by the time a kayaker reaches this point on the long run from the distant put-ins upstream, all they are focused on is getting out of the water and relaxing. Bad assumption. There are plenty of wading anglers who careen to a stop in the gravel parking lot, gear up and fish the immediate area. It doesn't matter whether it is a weekday or weekend, there are always people here.

On the other hand, the reason this is a popular location is that there always seem to be plenty of fish. Therefore, wade into the water, skip the sandy section in front of the take-out and move to the opposite bank. Facing upstream, rocks line the right bank. Tie on a popper and carefully fish the weed beds. Walk slowly upstream, fishing cautiously around the edges and targeting all the rock structure sticking above the level of the water.

Do this all the way to 38.31733,-77.54221 where the grass beds end and the rocks thin out. With the bottom becoming mostly sand, focus on the shoreline structure. In fact, at the end of the last grass island, fish the log structure on the right and then move approximately 1/3 of the way into the center of the river. There is an unavoidable, deep channel that runs down the right bank. After fishing it, the only way to get by is to move back to the center and edge along the ridge running up the center. If you are not tall, this may be as far you can go along the right bank.

At a gage reading of 176 cfs, the water is approximately four feet deep along the ridge. Orient on the rock to the front and eventually you will get to where you can move left or right near 38.31825,-77.54260. Although the bottom remains sandy, there are plenty of rocks and ridges that hold smallmouth. Therefore, do not skip through quickly – instead, take the time to work the structure with an inclination towards the right bank and the deep water that pushed you to the ridge.

A half mile upstream at 38.31910,-77.54256, a small, unnamed creek joins the river on the right bank near a small grass peninsula that pokes weakly into the river. Approach cautiously and fish the edges. This is a very good place to employ top water presentations, including small poppers, grasshoppers and other floating lures.

At the mouth of the creek, a rock ridge stretches at a 45° angle towards the center. It is shallow enough to follow the ridge into the river, but the best spot to fish is immediately on the right next to the largest/first rock. If you throw upstream, there is a deep hole with a sheltered ledge to the right of the large rock and that is where the fish will be. Once you work that spot, start walking up the right bank while paying attention to the cuts between the parallel rock ridges that stretch into the upstream distance. This is an area where the river remains shallow, but the cuts, with boundaries marked by scattered rocks, run two to three feet deep.

After fishing the ridge, stay close the right bank and work the 30 yard stretch from the bank into the river. While everything on the left will sport a sandy bottom, the bank is the exact opposite. There are long jagged ridges of rocks covered with a carpet of underwater vegetation. The next 50 yards will be the end of your upriver walk, but it may be the best fishing you encounter.

Wade back to the first set of grass beds and walk across the river to the other side. While the fishing is not as good on that bank, there is one superior location where the grass ends and transitions into a deep hole underneath some dramatically overhanging trees near 38.317506,-77.543259. You have to stay in the center of the river to fish it since the bank is extremely deep. Hit that spot and then walk back to the parking lot.

The prospective upstream from the entry point at 176 cfs.

The grass beds are productive on the northern bank.

This is the view of the small peninsula that pokes into the river from the north.

Look for these rock ridges extending 45° from the shoreline to move to the center of the river.

Beyond the peninsula, it becomes easier to walk to the center of the river on the 45° ridges.

On the way back, move to the southern bank to fish this spot directly above the last shoreline grass bed. Shown at 192 cfs.

Downstream

The first thing to notice as you walk down the stairs next to the canoe slide is the broad expanse of brown sand that stretches for 50 yards from the ramp along the first set of grass islands. Ignore the river on the right where the sand is excessive and retains no redeeming fishy structure. Instead, walk out to the grass island in the middle and begin to fish down the left bank. Immediately on the other side of the grass island at 38.31356,-77.53930 there is a series of deep holes defined by rock ridges running at a 45° angle pointing north. Each cradles a deeper hole of two to three feet. Fish there. The strategy should be to walk down the center, fish to the left bank, and when you get closed out by the lake at the end of the islands, work back up, fishing closer to the bank. When you complete the round-trip, walk back across the river to the parking lot.

The largest immediate hole is on the downstream, upper left side of the first set of grass islands. It is defined by the grass and a long high rock that points into the actual complex of rocks and weeds. Downstream of the long rock, the sand kicks in again. You may be tempted to fish the channels that run between the islands. Since the bottom is mostly sand and the river quickly becomes shallow in the summer, it is a fool's strategy when there is better water a few steps to the north. In fact, if you have your GPS, the boundary between the good and the bad is a line that runs from 38.313743,-77.539675 to 38.312483,-77.538224. The good water is to the north and the bad water is to the south.

Fortunately, you can figure this out without a GPS. There is a long sandbar running parallel with the flow of the river that creates a natural dividing line. One strategy is to walk all the way down to the end of the sandbar and then continue in the shallow water for another 250 feet where the broad lake that closed you out working upstream from Motts Run reappears. The only reason to go down this far is that there is fishable structure within casting distance. When the water is still and clear, you can easily see the rock ridges and boulders far below the surface.

38.31178,-77.53707 represents the downstream limit of how far you should bother to go. That is where the last grass island is on the left bounded by a large rock on the right. While you can continue to walk down the river in the shallow, sandy area off to the right, it is just exercise – the fishing will not be good. Instead, once on the last grass island, point your rod towards the north shore. Your first target should be the 10 foot deep spot that lies off the left edge of the island. After fishing below the island, turn around, look back upstream and pick a path through the shallow water that lines the bank in search of the deep spots. As you move upstream be aware that there are three good, rocky areas that are separated by deep water. The first is at 38.31178,-77.53707. Fish into the shoreline along the ridge. Once done, walk south to the sandy area, turn right and walk north 150 feet to 38.312279,-77.537766. Head back to the northern bank into a 40 foot wide complex of good rocky and vegetated structure. Instead of walking directly back out to the sand, move as far upstream as you can to fish the noticeably deep water that creates the northern boundary of this rock complex.

Head to the sand again and walk to the upstream tip of the sandbar. Everything on the northern side of the sandbar is good fishing water. Thoroughly work the ridgelines and cuts that lead to the shore. At normal levels, the water can be deep along the northern bank and you may find yourself unable to wade in the water close to the trees. That should not be a problem since there are plenty of ridges clawing their way to the bank that offer good perches for fishing.

This is the view from the base of the canoe launch. It is all sand downstream as far as you can see on the right-hand bank.

This is the downstream middle limit of the wadeable section. Once you visit this rock, you will not be able to go any farther.

This is the lower left limit of the fishable area at 176 cfs. Note the grass islands in the distance.

Looking upstream to the northern bank, you can see the rock ridge just under the surface of the water that defines the path to fish the deep spot just upstream.

Ignore the channels between the grass islands when the water is at summer low levels.

A view of one of the deeper areas on the northern bank. The rocks define the pathway to reach the better spots.

Bottom Line

The area around Clore Brothers is heavily fished. However, many people waste time targeting the islands and their sandy environments. If you walk a little farther up or downstream and know where to go, there are plenty of fish to catch in this area.

The Confluence

Google Map Coordinates: 38.36767,-77.618022

Summary Rating

Parking	**Red**	Spin Fishing	**Green**
Canoe/Kayak Launch	**Red**	Fly Fishing	**Green**
Distance to River	**Red**	Smallmouth Structure	**Green**
Can Bike to River	**Green**	Wading Distance	**Green**
Physical Fitness	**Red**	Pressure	**Yellow**
Scenery	**Green**	Overall	**Green**

There is no better fishing location for smallmouth bass in Virginia than the confluence of the Rapidan and the Rappahannock. All of the "red" ratings are actually positive factors that contribute to reducing the pressure. Most of the other anglers in the confluence float to this location on a canoe or a kayak. For those without a boat, the one mile walk down the moderate hill to reach the river filters out much of the other potential pressure.

Getting to the Stream

From I-95, merge onto VA 3 west at Fredericksburg and follow it for just under 9 miles. Turn right on Elys Ford Road (VA 610), go across the Rapidan and continue four miles. Turn right on Richards Ferry Road (VA 619) and follow it to the end. A thousand feet before the end, the road splits. Take the right fork. Park on the right side of the road at the end (38.382053,-77.625339). There are "no parking" signs on the opposite side to keep it clear so there will be room to turn around and get out.

At the end of the cul-de-sac, go past the gate on the City of Fredericksburg trail that leads to their campsite on the river (38.374871,-77.619481). Immediately prior to the campsite, the trail lurches right to move downstream. Take that fork and walk another 0.5 mile to get to the Confluence. The trail ends at the campsite that sits at the junction of the two rivers (38.368276,-77.619395).

Canoe/Kayak Comment: There is no launch point within a reasonable distance of the river. From the parking area at the end of Richards Ferry Road, it is a half mile to the river. Likewise, there is no take-out at the confluence itself. The closest put-in is at the Rappahannock River Campground and the next take-out is at the Clore Brothers parking lot.

Environment and Fish

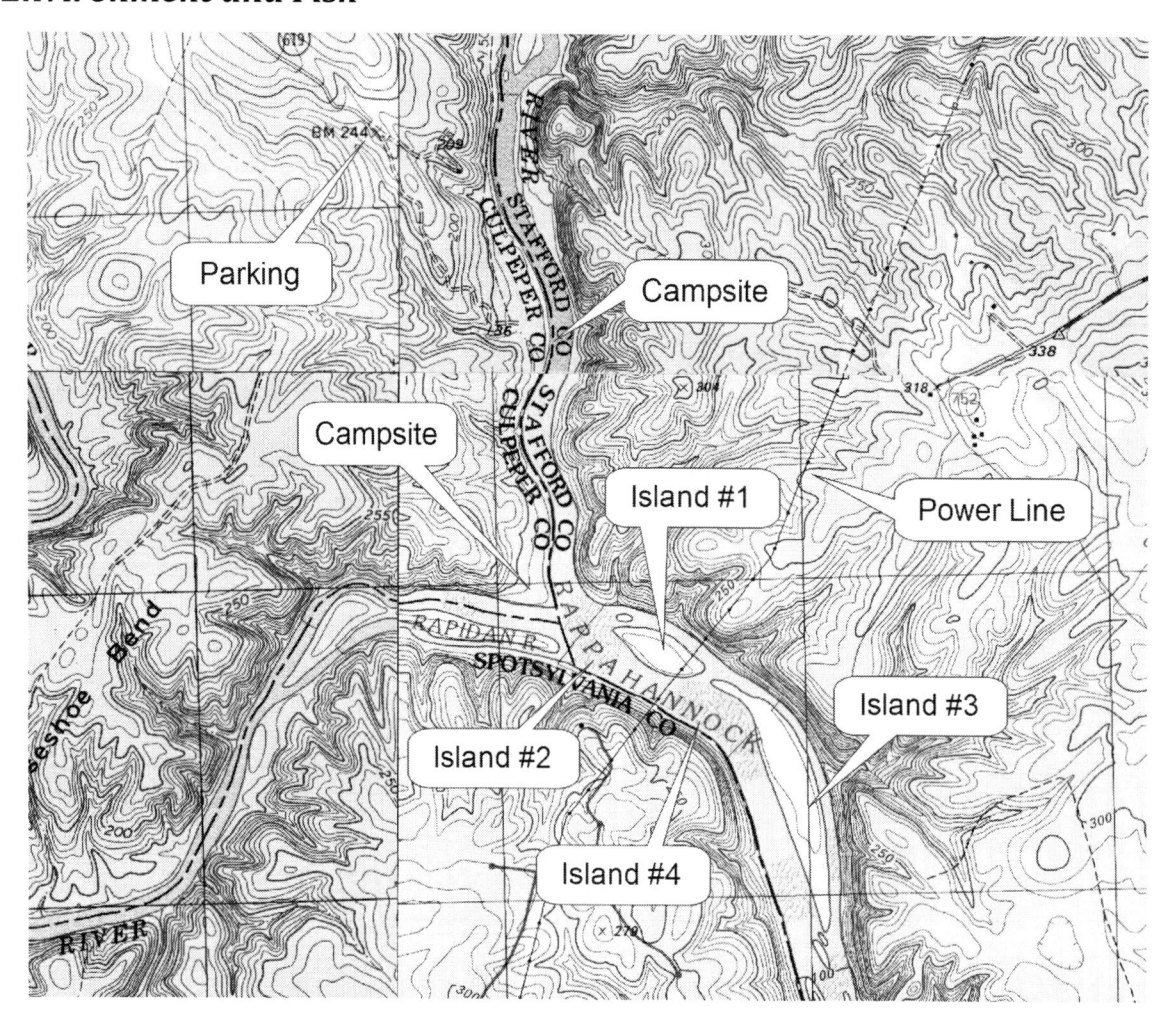

Without a doubt, the Confluence is the best place to fish for smallmouth bass in the entire Rappahannock and Rapidan River network. The Confluence is a jumble of boulders, slick ledges, channels and pools that conspire to create the perfect habitat for smallmouth and the ideal fishing destination for anyone willing to make the walk to the junction or float a kayak or canoe from upriver.

The trail from the parking area is an easy downhill walk and not a bad climb on the way back out. It will be an exercise in self-discipline to ignore the roar of the Rappahannock on the left as you keep your sights focused on the ultimate goal. However, as soon as you arrive at the tip of land (38.368276,-77.619395) that marks the junction of the two rivers and can gaze upstream at the Rappahannock on the left or the Rapidan to the right, as well as absorb the panorama of jumbled structure downstream where the two rivers crash together, whatever sweat it cost to get here is instantly worth it. In fact, you may have a nervous breakdown on the spot generated by an overwhelming wave of uncertainty about where to start. You are truly the kid in a candy store with a pocket full of cash and everything on sale. It is just that good!

All of the water downstream of where you stand is in the Rappahannock. There are actually two sections of the Confluence - the one just in front of you and the "lower Confluence" that starts three quarters of a mile downstream (38.360638,-77.610319).

That said, you have days of fishing spread out in front of you. To completely exploit the Confluence will take several trips. The best way to deal with it is to execute a search pattern that starts on the right running in parallel bands starting from north to south. The reason to start on the right is simple. As you look left, there is a side channel separated from the northern shoreline by a large, grassy island (38.367031,-77.615962 - Island #1). Up until the end of July, plenty of water fills the channel and it creates a "mini-river" all by itself. Since it is narrow, the best approach is to head upstream. Therefore, leave that section to the end of the day as you work back up to the trailhead to hike back to your vehicle.

Start fishing in the deep pools to the left as you enter the river from the tip of the campsite. Fish carefully because earlier in the year large smallmouth congregate near the campsite. It is after the campsite has been visited repeatedly by canoeists and kayakers making the overnight voyage down to Fredericksburg that these fish wise up and go elsewhere. As soon as you step off the bank, you find yourself in a wide open area marked by small tufts of grass clinging to the tops of a convoluted jumble of dense boulder structure that represents a nightmare to boaters as they try to work their way through the junction. Their agony is your joy as each represents a channel leading to a pool and every pool holds fish. Granted, you can catch sunfish anywhere you throw a lure in the Confluence. These feisty fish aggressively attack anything that is small enough to get into their mouths. Therefore, you should upsize your terminal tackle unless you actually want to catch them.

If you are hunting for a larger fish, focus on pools that are least three feet deep. At the start of the season, the big boys penetrate into the shallower water, but at the height of summer they move to the deeper pools or rest in the shade along the shoreline.

Once you fish the area in the immediate vicinity of the tip, point your rod south and fish across the mouth of the Rapidan to the southern shoreline. There is a large blowdown of jumbled logs that shelters some deep water that should get some casts. As you fish around it, the blowdown should also be a lesson regarding the power of the river at full flood. The massive fallen tree that forms the base of the jumble was pushed here from upstream when the river was at high flow. It is a visible example of why you must know the gage reading to ensure that you are not about to step into a torrent of water and risk death by drowning.

Once past the blowdown, look downstream to the small island (38.366745,-77.617282 - Island #2) that divides the river into two sections. Island #1 is to the left, the shoreline is to the right with a narrow channel running around the right side of Island #2. Fish to Island #2 and continue down the southern channel between it and the shore. Eventually, you will see the old rock wall of the canal where the river picks up some speed as it grinds against the shoreline. There are some good pools over on that side and you should fish those as you work all the way down to the slack water that occurs upstream of the power lines (38.365481,-77.615372). The power lines represent a critical boundary. They are about 500 yards downstream of the campsite. If you continue farther downstream, you will have a longer, tougher walk back to your vehicle. Therefore, if you feel tired, fish up the southern side of Island #1 or walk to the other side and fish the tight channel that embraces the northern shoreline to complete your search pattern.

If you fish up the south side of Island #1, stay to the middle of the channel between it and Island #2 (38.366745,-77.617282). That area holds the deepest water and the possibility of larger fish. If the flow is good enough, and you decide to go to the other side of Island #1, do not start fishing upstream immediately from the downstream tip of the island. Instead, walk another 200 yards downstream to the tip of yet another, even larger island (38.364104,-77.610555 - Island #3) that compresses the side channel into a narrow band about 30 feet wide. The reason is that the 200 yards you would have skipped is a maze of "deeper" two to three foot holes with channels leading into them. From the tip of Island #3, fish upstream targeting the northern shoreline. You can easily pick up 20 fish in this section floating poppers against the rocks and over the channels.

Finish the 200 yard section and continue along the northern shoreline where the river narrows and pools at the base of three distinct gradient breaks (one is at the power line, the next is 150 feet upstream and the final is at the tip of the island). Each represents an opportunity to catch a larger fish. After fishing the first two breaks moving upstream, there is a narrow band of trees separating Island #1 from the northern shoreline. At lower water levels, you can flip a coin to decide which side to fish, but I prefer the northern side because it is wider and offers deeper pools. At the upstream tip of the island, there is a large, obvious ridge of rocks that separates this entire geographic structure from the main part of the river. Fish the pools and return to the campsite.

Early morning fog shrouds the confluence looking upstream to the junction.

View downstream towards the junction from the Rapidan at 290 cfs.

View upstream - Island #2 is to the right. The river is running at 638 cfs.

This is the confluence at its finest. The numerous grass islands, channels and rocks all work together to create the optimum smallmouth bass environment.

Another view of the great structure in the confluence looking upstream towards the junction from the power line.

Be prepared to catch massive smallmouth at the confluence. This guy (21") hit a small blue popper floated next to log near island #3.

Power Line Downstream

If you have the energy, you may want to walk directly to the power line and start fishing there. Your target for the day is the section of rapids immediately downstream of the power line and the western shore of Island #3 at river left. The river is deepest in the vicinity of the power line. Fish either side of the small island (38.365567,-77.613859 - Island #4) that is the key terrain feature breaking the river into two sections upstream of Island #3. Looking downstream at the bottom of Island #4, the part of the river between it and Island #3 is mostly shallow. Continue to fish downstream on river right until abreast of the tip of Island #3.

Walk over to Island #3 and fish its western shoreline. After experiencing the great water between Island #1 and the northern shoreline, you might assume the character of the river would be similar between Island #3 and the shoreline. Do not bother. The river goes slack and the bottom turns into sand. If you poke your nose in that direction, you will have a 500 yard walk with nothing to show for it. That said, I have had friends find some decent fish there. I write that off to luck and confused fish taking a wrong turn.

The bottom of Island #3 marks the boundary of what I consider to be the Confluence. An additional walk puts you on the next section - the lower Confluence.

This is the view downstream looking towards island #3 from the power line.

Midway alongside island #3 facing downstream at 638 cfs.

This is the view upstream at the gap between island #1 and #3. The deep channel is on the right near the shore.

Downstream into the gap between island #3 and the shoreline. Do not fish beyond the gap since the river gets shallow and sandy. Concentrate on the water from the tip of island #3 upstream.

View downstream into the structure on the right side of island #3.

Upstream towards the power line from island #3.

The Lower Confluence

The lower confluence is far enough from the junction to merit its own map. Fair warning, if you set your sights on fishing here, it is a two-mile walk from the city campground. On the other hand, it is only a couple hundred feet upstream from the Blankenbakers put-in if you engage a shuttle or rent a canoe from Clore Brothers.

The Blankenbaker put-in is private. The road to reach the river runs through the Blankenbaker's front yard; you will not be able to go there on your own. If you are not capable of doing the 2 mile hike from the Richards Ferry Road access point, paying the Clore Brothers for the shuttle to this spot is well worth it. Not only do you get to fish a great section of the river, but you also can enjoy some superb fishing on the seven mile paddle back to the Clore Brothers take-out near Motts Run.

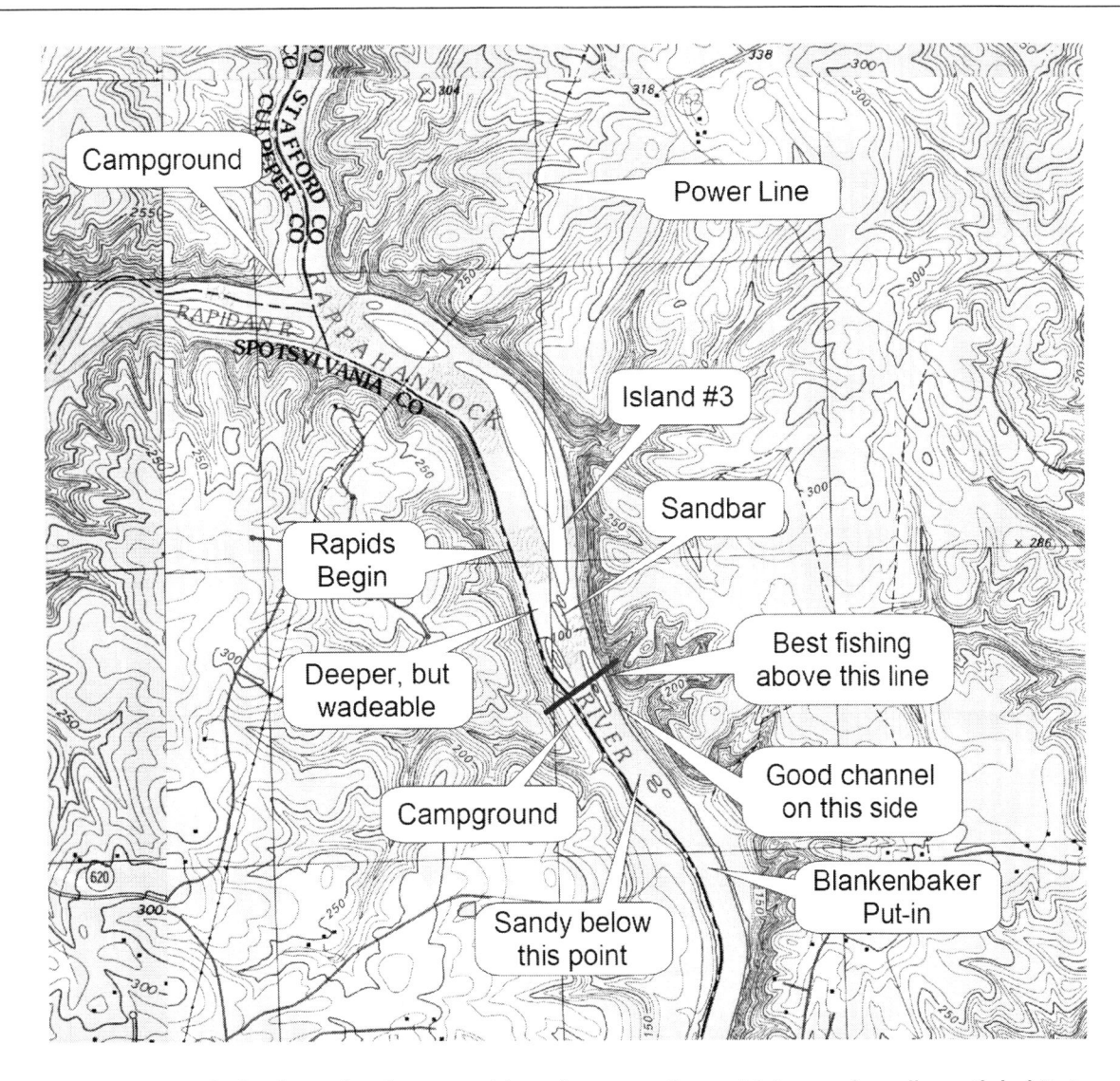

Map labels:
- Campground
- Power Line
- Island #3
- Sandbar
- Rapids Begin
- Deeper, but wadeable
- Best fishing above this line
- Good channel on this side
- Campground
- Blankenbaker Put-in
- Sandy below this point

At the lower tip of Island #3, the river transitions from mostly sand into good smallmouth habitat with the boundary being the very visible set of rapids that begins at 38.360366,-77.610255. I recommend that instead of starting there, you walk to the lower end of the fishable section and work upstream. You can do this very quickly by following Island #3 all the way to the sandbar that hangs off its end, skip across the hundred foot section of rapids to another sandbar that extends all the way down to 38.355436,-77.607117. Once there, the upstream chunk of the river is the best in the lower area. However, if you really have a lot of energy, you could continue to fish the shoreline all the way down to 38.353404,-77.60502 where there is another large sandbar complex on the right and a few small riffles. If you end up being parallel with the pipeline, you've gone too far. As a follow-up to comments I made in the chapter on the Clore Brothers access point, the pipeline gap is just upstream from the Blankenbakers put-in. If you want to fish the lower section, it is well worth paying the shuttle fee or renting a completely outfitted canoe from Clore Brothers to obtain access to this portion of the river without enduring the long hike from the city campground. In addition, after you fish this section, you can take the easy 7 mile float, fishing water that you cannot access otherwise, back to your car.

Taking the perspective of walking back to the city campground or up from the Blankenbakers put-in, ignore the left bank of the river (river right). While it is deep just ahead of the sandbar complex at 38.353404,-77.60502, the sand tends to overwhelm the quality of fishing. In the heat of the summer, this deep water offers a cool holding area for bass and provides the exception to what I just wrote. The bass will range out from the deep water in search of food along the shore or up into the well defined rapids upstream. Therefore, if it is hot and you do not find them anywhere else, come to this spot.

The right shore is a dense complex of overhanging trees and many fallen logs that wrap around good rocky habitat. The best way to fish upstream is to find a compatible underwater sandbar that allows you to move upstream without swimming. Fish to either side with most of your casts being towards the shore. The closer you get to the tree covered tip of the upstream sandbar, the more you need to be aware of what is on the left as well as the right. At the height of summer, the river on the left sandbar tends to become overgrown with vegetation. There are plenty of big fish lurking on that side, but unless you go weedless or fish the surface, you will be constantly tangled. On the other hand, the right side of the sandbar remains consistently free from clogging underwater vegetation. There is a channel that runs along the middle between the sandbar and the shoreline that is covered with underwater boulders and associated rocky structure.

Since the largest fish I have caught on the Rappahannock were pulled out of the section to the right of the sandbar, I recommend you fish upstream on that side first. Slow down and pay special attention to the deep run just below the gradient break at 38.356651,-77.607599. Stay on the right of the sandbar since it is shallow and sandy about 20 feet out in all directions. At the gradient break, leverage the sandbar to walk quickly back down to the tip and repeat your attack focused on the left side of the river. There are plenty of rocks and you need to be careful where you step because it is very deep in random places. There is a popular campsite on the beach at 38.3557,-77.608364, and the area directly in front of it gets more pressure than the run on the northern side of the sandbar.

If you were to draw a line from the tip of the sandbar horizontally across the river between 38.356104,-77.608598 and 38.356727,-77.607525, that line describes the start of the best 500 feet for fishing in the area. In fact, it is all so good that all I can do is tell you about is the one place you should not go. Do not wander back into the few channels that dribble behind the island complex on the left bank (38.356104,-77.60859). At higher water levels, you might pick up a fish or two back there, but with all the other spectacular water just to the right, it is not worth the effort. You can split your approach using the northern extension of the sandbar as the landmark to guide your effort. Above that imaginary line, there are two small lakes, one on either side of the sandbar that have deeper water and more fish. Beyond those, the river fractures into a tortured succession of rocks, ridges and the associated channels with deep spots. Anywhere you fish between the imaginary line and the downstream tip of Island #3 at 38.358052,-77.608919 is going to be so good that you will not want to walk back to your canoe and deal with the 7 mile paddle back to the Clore Brothers take-out.

Once at the tip, do not make the mistake of fishing up the right channel around the Island #3. There is not enough flow to push the sand downstream. Sand equates to bad bass habitat. Besides, why bother when you have all the good water, with plenty of rocks and the minimum of sand, on the western side of Island #3? As you fish, some of the holes become deep and will close you out. Move back towards Island #3 or the shore to work around those spots. Within this short, 250 foot section, there are four defined ridges that run across the river:

- 38.359364,-77.610046
- 38.359776,-77.609965
- 38.360163,-77.610046
- 38.360413,-77.610265

Each ridge has a corresponding good up and downstream section. You do not need a GPS to find them, you just need to be aware that they are there so you do not waste time fishing in the sandy, marginal areas. Move towards the middle of the river or the left bank and do not spend much time on the right bank that comprises the lower tip of Island #3.

The view upstream from the top at 1,050 cfs – you can see the power line in the distance.

This area is replete with good, wide channels - full of rocks and fish.

The area is full of fast-moving water splashing across perpendicular ledges.

If you do not catch at least one guy like this, you had a real bad day. Caught and released - as usual. - please do the same.

My personal favorite is the channel opposite the campground on the north side of the narrow spit of land.

Another good set of ledges.

Bottom Line

Although I just attempted to do it, words cannot describe the Confluence. While there is good fishing elsewhere on the Rappahannock River, the Confluence represents a model of perfection for smallmouth habitat that cannot be duplicated.

Richards Ferry Road - City Campsite

Google Map Coordinates: 38.375874,-77.619173

Summary Rating

Parking	**Red**	Spin Fishing	**Green**
Canoe/Kayak Launch	**Red**	Fly Fishing	**Green**
Distance to River	**Red**	Smallmouth Structure	**Green**
Can Bike to River	**Green**	Wading Distance	**Green**
Physical Fitness	**Yellow**	Pressure	**Yellow**
Scenery	**Green**	Overall	**Green**

This is an overlooked location. Most people assume that since there is a campsite, this section receives heavy pressure. While that may be true directly in front of the campsite, there always seems to be plenty of fish to hold an angler's interest. If you are hard-core and walk upstream, you will not be disappointed with the quality of the water at the far end of your hike.

Getting to the Stream

From I-95, merge onto VA 3 west at Fredericksburg and follow it for just under 9 miles. Turn right on Elys Ford Road (VA 610), go across the Rapidan and continue four miles. Turn right on Richards Ferry Road (VA 619) and follow it to the end. A thousand feet before the end, the road splits. Take the right fork. Park on the right side of the road at the end (38.382053,-77.625339). There are "no parking" signs on the opposite side to keep it clear so there will be room to turn around and get out.

Go through the gate (picture) that marks the City easement to the campsite and follow the easy trail to the river. Immediately prior to reaching the river, the trail splits. Take the left hand fork towards the campsite. The other fork goes to the Confluence.

Canoe/Kayak Comment: There is no easy access for launching a boat at this point. It is a half mile walk from the parking lot to the river.

Environment and Fish

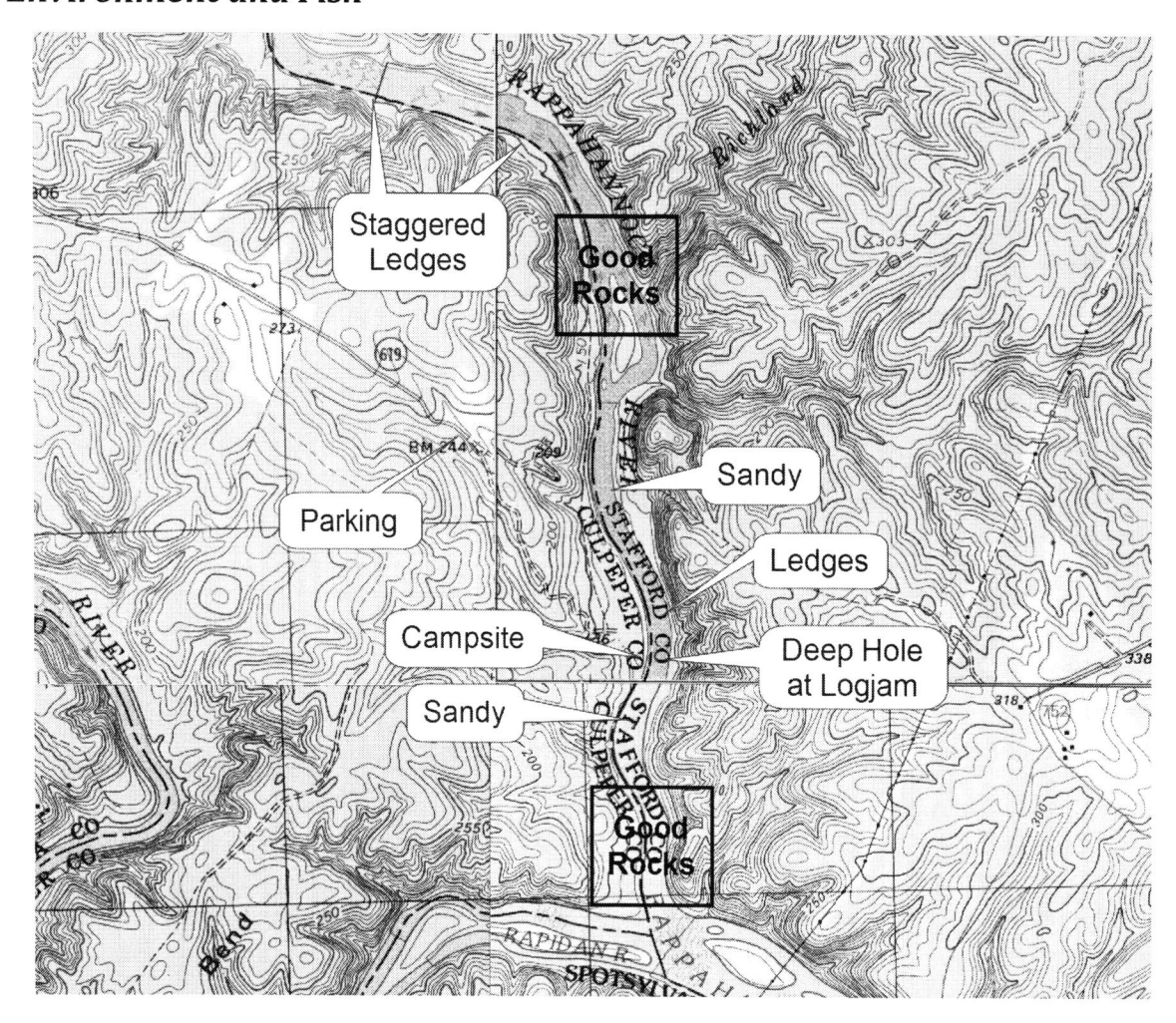

Upstream

Use the Remington gage from here upriver.

Upon arrival at the city campsite at 38.37526,-77.619494, do not make the mistake of believing you need to walk farther upstream before fishing. You have already put a half mile between yourself and the parking lot and, by itself, that is a compelling filter on pressure. Even though this is a popular campsite for those who canoe or kayak from points upstream, the area immediately in front of the campsite offers some of the best fishing in this section.

Slide down the steep hill and walk towards the ledge of rocks that lies to the right front. Ignore the small complex of rocks and runs immediately downstream from the campsite and turn to the upstream jumble of shoreline vegetation that forms the outer perimeter of a deep pool. At normal water levels in the summer, you will not be able to wade more than 10 feet away from the ledge. Take a long cast into the tangle of logs and be patient while your lure sinks to the bottom. That complex is "infested." Be prepared to catch one of the huge carp that cruise this area. From the ledge upstream 1,000 feet, you may see their huge bodies gliding silently under the water, sometimes followed by a gaggle of smallmouth scavenging whatever the carp kick up. When done, walk back to the shore.

Your upriver strategy is simple. Ignore the left bank and focus on the right. To do that, find a line that represents a comfortable depth to wade and begin to walk upstream. For the next quarter mile, there are a series of slick ledges that extend up to the eastern shore. Wherever you find one, move to the shore and target the deep water above and below it. Do not go fast and do not ignore anything. The most significant set of ledges starts at 38.376244,-77.618575 and extends upstream to finally transition back to a sandy bottom at 38.377389,-77.61887 where you are approximately 1,000 feet upstream from the campsite.

The next 400 feet of the river is mostly sandy bottom; although there are a few small ledges and boulders that, if you are lucky, may hold fish. I recommend you walk directly through the bad water to get to the first significant new ledge that marks the start of the short 200 foot section of good water between 38.378269,-77.619385 and 38.379083,-77.620072. Good is a relative term since the water is not as optimal as it is near the campsite. Depending on your energy levels, the real upstream target is the faster water with twisted channels and small pools that extends for 2,000 feet upstream from 38.381305,-77.62086.

Once there, switch your focus from the right bank to the left, moving closer to the right bank to fish the fast water that swings around the wide S-curve upstream. There is a large sandbar at 38.383076,-77.620206 that forces the water into a tight run just south of an island. You have two choices at the island - move up the left channel or swing around to the right where the water is deeper, but sandy. In either case, cross the river wherever you can find a shallow path between the sandbar and the island.

If the water levels are a little bit higher, the left channel can be productive, but it tends to shallow up in the summer. Therefore, the better, consistent strategy is to move to the right and hit the deeper water upstream of the sandbar. While the bottom is mostly sand, there are some rocks and ledges that provide shelter for fish. If you get anxious about skipping the channel, fish it as you return. I know I'm pushing you to walk an extended distance at this point, but since you are already this far, you owe it to yourself to fish the logs and ledges that collect north of the upstream tip of the island. In particular, everything between the tip of the island at 38.386412,-77.620234 and 38.387842,-77.620867 is good. When you stand at 38.387842,-77.620867, you are approximately a mile upstream of the campsite and that puts you 1.5 miles from your vehicle.

This is a good place to turn around because while there are four additional ledge complexes upstream, they are separated by sand and demand a concerted effort to slog upstream against the current. Just to complete the story, those ledges are located at:

- 38.389577,-77.621931
- 38.391275,-77.62427
- 38.391982,-77.627038
- 38.392436,-77.630106

The best one is the last one. Fair warning – the last ledge is 1.5 miles from the campsite and two miles from your vehicle. I need to apologize here – my camera failed on the trip I took to document this stretch. I only have a few shots that are not very informative.

This is the view back to the city campground from upriver.

Farther up river at 42 cfs.

Downstream

If you want to fish downstream from the city campsite, the best strategy is to walk directly to the confluence and fish upstream. Fortunately, it is a very easy half mile hike on a level trail to reach the tip of the confluence. Once there, you will have second thoughts. The pull of the confluence is irresistible and, no doubt, you will find yourself spending an hour or two hitting all of the great water I discussed in the previous chapter before you swing your rod back upstream.

The first thousand feet upstream from the junction is a mixture of isolated small pools created by the infinite number of channels shaped by the random, scattered ledges and rocks that make walking difficult. In fact, you could become disoriented and think you are still in the actual confluence. The key difference is that the ledges are smaller and not as obvious. There are fewer tall rocks poking above the surface of the water to provide landmarks and orientation. As a general statement, the main, deep flow ends up being on the right bank.

One way to orient yourself is to focus on the small amount of visible structure that lies upstream. Anywhere you see a tall rock stretching towards the sky is the location of a deep spot that will protect the larger fish. In particular, focus on 38.369421,-77.618913 (300 feet upstream from the tip) and 38.370802,-77.618764 (1,000 feet upstream). You do not need a GPS to find these rocks, they are obvious. From the upper one, you still have another 200 feet of good fishing to enjoy before reaching the lower boundary of the "sand zone" that extends the rest of the way up to the city campsite.

There is a minor rock formation usually visible at 38.371868,-77.619117. It is the transition point into the sand. As you fish up to that point, the right bank continues to be the best choice, but do not forget to fish the pool just upstream as the rocks peter out and the sand begins. Throw your rod on your shoulder and do not bother with anything else until you move to the sandbar at the corner of the river. Walk up the center of the sandbar and the rocks come into view in the channel that runs down the middle of the river (38.373843,-77.61976). Frankly, it is not worth spending much time in this particular spot since you are only 100 feet away from the good hole that borders the city campsite. Once at the campsite, you can make the call on whether to continue to fish upstream for the next couple of hundred feet to take advantage of the ridges and the carp that hang out in the deep water on the right bank.

Immediately upstream of the confluence a jumbled, random maze of rock structure predominates.

If you find a good channel in this confusion, you can find good fish at 120 cfs.

This is the lake adjacent to the campsite

There is a good spot to the right as you walk up the small drop in elevation that leads to the campsite.

Bottom Line

If you can ignore the confluence just downstream, you can have a good day between the Confluence and the island a mile upstream from the campsite. This is a good place for a quick trip since a short walk down the hill drops you on the good water next to the campsite. You could easily spend an hour or two fishing and that single location.

Rappahannock River Campground

Google Map Coordinates: 38.41614,-77.662611

Summary Rating

Parking	Green	Spin Fishing	Green
Canoe/Kayak Launch	Green	Fly Fishing	Green
Distance to River	Yellow	Smallmouth Structure	Green
Can Bike to River	Red	Wading Distance	Green
Physical Fitness	Yellow	Pressure	Yellow
Scenery	Green	Overall	Green

Do not write off the Rappahannock River Campground as a potential fishing location because you suspect it is highly pressured. While there is pressure in the immediate vicinity of the canoe take-out, a quick walk up or downstream puts you on very good water. Upstream leads to a confluence-like section that is sprinkled with dense vegetation, rocky outcroppings and the associated narrow, twisted channels creating great hiding structure. A quick walk a half mile downstream leads to deep water protecting boulder fields and the larger bass that migrate there to escape the summer heat.

Getting to the Stream

From I-95, merge onto VA 3 west at Fredericksburg and follow it for just under 9 miles. Turn right on Elys Ford Road (VA 610), go across the Rapidan and continue four miles. Turn right on Richards Ferry Road (VA 619) and follow it for 2.6 miles. Turn left on River Mill Rd (VA 683) and go to the end.

Once you park in the open field near the camp store and pay the access fee, take a short 0.2 mile stroll down the gently sloping hill behind the store, go across the field and enter the river.

Canoe/Kayak Comment: The Rappahannock River Campground is all about canoeing and kayaking. They have a well-built, improved launch that includes a slide to make it easy to get a boat in or out of the water.

Environment and Fish

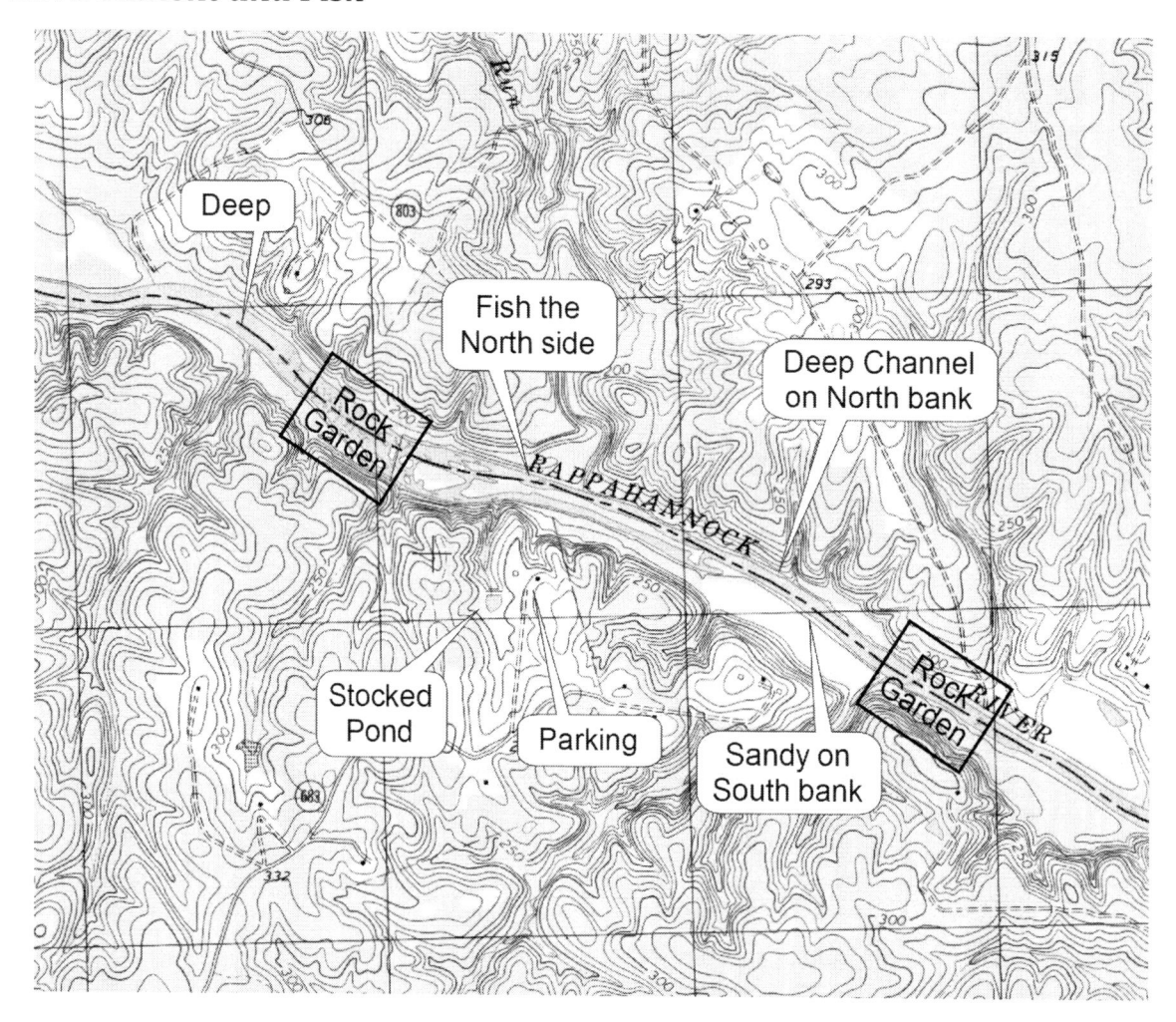

Map labels: Deep; Fish the North side; Deep Channel on North bank; Rock Garden; Stocked Pond; Parking; Sandy on South bank; Rock Garden

The quality of fishing in the vicinity of the Rappahannock River Campground will stun you. The instant, and wrong, conclusion you may have come to when you read the chapter heading is that since the river borders a popular campground, the fishing must be horrible. While it is pressured, most of the people who visit this spot are more interested in camping and canoeing than taking a hike up or downriver to go fishing. Walk a couple of hundred yards and you are home free. Granted, you have to deal with waves of canoes at the height of the season in April, May and June as they slide into the finish line after a long float, but there are a profusion of places separated from the traffic that hold plenty of fish. Besides, it takes hours for all those trips to make it back to the take-out, thereby guaranteeing peace in the early morning.

Joyfully, there are two extremely good choices. You can walk up into a confluence–like rock garden and fish as far upriver as you have the energy to go or head a half mile downriver to work over a lightly pressured, ideal stretch of the river.

Upstream

After walking down the canoe ramp (pictured), move directly across the river to the gap that splits the long island at 38.418668,-77.662698.

Walk through the gap to reach the main channel of the river on the north side. In the upstream distance, a jumbled moonscape of confusing, convoluted rock beckons. Head in that direction.

If you need to warm up, exploit the deep channel that runs next to the northern bank. Fish the cut next to the fallen tree opposite the first grassy point and then prepare to get busy as you enter the rock garden. Beyond the gap, the left bank is not interesting even though it features thick grass beds. There is not enough depth to make it attractive to fish except during the early morning and late evening when the fish feed at the perimeter of the vegetation.

If you need to turn around, there is a gap in the island at 38.418988,-77.665031 that leads back to the shallow southern channel and the campground. In fact, when the wind is right, this is where you will be tortured by the comforting smell of open campfires and, if early, the warm scent of cooking bacon moving through the still air. After all, anything cooked over a campfire is both calorie and cholesterol free!

At 38.41910,-77.66351, 150 feet up from the gap, you finally enter the rock garden. Early in the year when the water levels are higher, it is worth fishing the downstream section below the first line of rocks that reach completely across the river. Do not ignore the river immediately upstream since the water backs up and collects over a good complex of jagged rocks. Fish by moving around to the left to exploit the entire spot. When done, you stand at the key landmark, a narrow spit of land that points downstream like the tip of a spear. When there is water present, it is worth fishing the right channel for the next 200 feet all the way up to 38.41968,-77.66619.

When the water is low ignore the right side since it will get clogged with grass, and focus on the left. Skip the first 20 feet until you pass a large fallen tree. Slide into the current and target the deep pool immediately upstream, allocating extra time to the log that stretches across the river.

Beyond the hole, enter the rock garden. The fishing will be situational depending on the weather and the water level. As a capstone strategy, I recommend remaining in the rock garden to fish up the right side of the river, following the main stream of the current on that side. Then, fish back to the camp by following the channel that runs along the southern shore. That way, you will not miss the exit point and will have covered the entire area.

Fishing the rock garden is a matter of picking a channel or pool, creeping up without making too much noise, and making your presentation. A key feature in the heart of the rock garden is the lake at 38.419606,-77.666766. The spot remains consistently deep in the summer and is open enough to hold fish underneath the densely packed grass bed that lines the shore. Wind through the channels, staying to the left of the huge tangle of logs at the front, until breaking out of the rock garden at 38.420071,-77.668365. Before moving any further, fish the deep hole at the transition point. Since the grass does not come all the way to the surface of the water, it is a good place to throw casts using a fan pattern starting from the left and working all the way around to the right.

Early in the year, it is worthwhile to work up the right side to fish all the small cuts and runs that crater out in two foot deep pools. In the middle of summer, the grass grows high enough to choke all the small channels. While a fish may still be there, fishing will be extremely difficult and not worth the effort. Instead of wasting time on the right side of the island, walk up the left to the tip at 38.41961,-77.668515. Looking upriver, the deep water starts upstream of the large logjam to the right front. These sections have the perfect amount of grass cover to support forage, but remain open enough to fish effectively. The best way to get to them is to walk straight upstream from the Rappahannock River Campground sign (put there to orient river traffic to the take-out) and look to the right. That is where the deep sections are with the first occurring in front of the logjam (38.420119,-77.668743) and the second about 25 yards upstream (38.420497,-77.66933). When you identify one of these spots, fish it by moving back to the right bank, instead of just from the left edge. Each deep section borders a higher ridgeline that allows lateral movement. Zigzag up to the top of the next ridgeline and repeat that same attack pattern.

By the time you reach 38.42066,-77.66986, at the base of a set of rocks poking above the surface that runs perpendicular to the flow, you should have fished back and forth on four such deep channels (38.420102,-77.668759, 38.420518,-77.669282, 38.420665,-77.669585, 38.420804,-77.669762) with the last two tending to blend into one. If it gets too deep, work back to the left (southern) bank of the river (where it stays shallow) and move upstream from there.

At 38.42066,-77.66986, you may feel a little panic after fishing all of the channels when all that is apparent upstream is a fast current running over a shallow bed. Do not worry. Not 20 yards upstream from the small gradient break, there is another extraordinarily deep channel running between a grass island and a set of rocks followed by a twin channel extending all the way across the river. Position yourself on the left bank and walk up the shallow shelf. Look for the dark green shade of water and, as it comes into view, move across the rock ridge to fish the entire stretch.

The farther you move upriver, the more frequent the deep channels become. If the water is at acceptable levels for canoeing, you probably will not be able to wade this far upriver. Granted, the left bank is reasonably shallow, so walk upriver throwing towards the center, but to really exploit it demands being here when the water is at summer lows. 38.42130,-77.67083 is another deep area where the channels weave between a few scattered rock islands that provide the boundary perimeter for submerged ledges hanging under six feet of water.

Pick a careful path to move onto a large flat rock that overlooks the key channel and fish from there. By the time you reach the rock, you are 0.6 miles from your vehicle. Since this is the end of the rock garden, it is a good place to turn around and fish the good channel that hugs the southern bank.

On the way back to the canoe slide, follow the current along with the left bank (southern bank). Follow the directional arrow on the sign nailed to the tree to enter the narrow cut leading back to the campground. As soon as you pass the tree, you could easily imagine yourself on a California trout stream. The current is tight, spinning around boulders and charging down channels to energetically shoot over the deep holes. Be sure you have enough energy left to fish this section instead of crashing through on the way back to your vehicle.

Once through the gap, head upstream towards the large tree. It divides the river into two channels (71 cfs).

Fish up the left-hand channel to the fallen tree.

Once above the split island, the rock garden opens up.

There are an infinite number of good places to fish tucked into this small piece of terrain.

Use this logjam as the landmark as you execute a grid pattern to cover the entire section.

Above the rock garden, the river breaks out into a series of perpendicular channels, each outlined by a rock ridge.

This is the first perpendicular channel at the outer edge of the dense rock garden.

The left-hand bank features a lake area – It is shallow near the tree line so you can fish around the entire feature.

This is one of the last perpendicular channels prior to hitting the unwadeable section upstream.

The river starts to look like a trout stream as you follow the side channel back to the campground.

Downstream

The initial perspective looking downstream is not good. Before you panic, realize that you stand in a low-volume side channel to the main river. Just like I described earlier, you could walk through the cut and have a good day fishing downstream. The better choice is to use the sandy bottom of the side channel as an easy walking highway to move a half mile downstream to the lower tip of the long island (38.416387,-77.654683). From there, you can make the decision on whether you want to immediately fish back upstream or continue down. My description assumes you fish farther downriver and then follow the main channel all the way back up to the gap where you can cut across to the campground. If you only want to fish back to the campground, skip ahead in the story.

Approach the tip of the island warily. The water is deep and this is the first place to target. Specifically, stand back a little bit from the edge of the sand and fish directly upstream along the left bank. There is a large sunken log that holds as many sunfish and a few good sized smallmouth bass. Once done, fish from left to right to complete the circle around the end of the sandbar. I know, you have to ignore the sound of rushing water and dramatic rocks just upstream, but it is pretty good heading in the other direction as well.

Hopefully, after catching a number of fish off the sandbar, the initial disappointment you felt when you stepped off the canoe ramp has evaporated. Do not expect a confluence here. The attraction of this section is that it consists of enough rocks and ledges to make the area interesting to smallmouth along with the cool, deep water they seek on hot summer days. Combine that with the good overhanging vegetation from the northern bank and you have the recipe for success.

As soon as you step off the sandbar, you discover that the water is pretty deep – even at summer lows. Pick a careful path along the scattered ridges that stretch perpendicular to the flow within the first 100 feet of the junction. I recommend you find the first one that allows you to get all the way to the northern bank. Fish to the bank warily to exploit the deep water and the shade underneath the trees. Depending on the water levels, you may not be able to move very far downstream on the northern bank. If closed out, hug the right bank to continue downstream to the logjam.

While you cannot see it from the center of the river, if you walk over to the left bank, there is a grass bed growing out from the bank approximately 20 feet into the river. The grass nestles large boulders and small minnows skitter as you approach. It is a little shallower next to the bank and that becomes the avenue to move farther downstream. Fish the beds as you go since nice smallmouth huddle at the drop off marking the transition from shallow to deep.

After fishing the grass, you may feel like you can move directly back to the center of the river. It does shallow out about 20 yards down from where you hit the bank, but the center is pockmarked with deep, deep holes that prevent downstream wading even at the height of summer. Therefore, continue to walk down the left bank and enjoy the optimum smallmouth bass habitat along the shore. Huge rock ridges stretch to the center, terminating in a boulder field of medium sized chunks of rock. With grass growing from every crack, this area is full of food! Move cautiously while throwing poppers and catching fish. The most significant terrain feature is the large tree that stretches over the river just downstream of the major fallen log. There are some deep holes underneath it that protect the fish. Do not blunder downstream without fishing in every direction. In short, this spot is infested with bass.

At the tree, fish underneath its broad protective base, then walk back a few feet to the ridge of rocks that runs perpendicular to the river. Use this to move into the center where the water continues to be "sporty", but you need to be alert for the shallow and deep areas. From there, move downstream with continued attention on the left bank - the right bank is uninteresting. However, if the river is murky and you cannot see the bottom, you should not try this because there are plenty of boulders that will cause you to trip. Beyond that, you need to be able to see the shallow areas, using them to guide your movement, to avoid the deep holes that predominate.

Beyond the trees at 38.41571,-77.65283, the density of rocks decreases and the amount of sand increases. The deep channel remains on the left bank and, where you can wade within casting distance, it is worth fishing into the shade. Adding interest, a few rock ridges run perpendicular to the river. Unless you find a deep spot, the center is boring. All of the action is on the bank in and around the vegetation.

If you are reading this book, you are a hard-core smallmouth angler, and I know you have had your eye on the distant downstream grass beds. They are a mile from the entry point and are the downstream extent of your wading. As you approach them, the river switches from sand back to rock with the left bank being the one to target. In the approach into the grassy island area, the river shallows out, the sand decreases and the amount of grass on the periphery of the river increases.

At 38.41373,-77.64883, the grass area begins. While the bank is too shallow to hold much of anything on the left, if you follow the main channel of the river, it runs over the deep sections. There is a small lake just downstream of the large rock that splits the river into three channels with the main flow moving around the grass bed immediately downstream. Cautiously approach the lake from behind the rock and, using it for cover, throw into the lake area. From the rock, cast downstream into the pool as close to the left bank as you can reach, but do not spend too much time here because the real prize is beyond the two grass islands that form the downstream border of the first pool. Circle around, following the current on the right bank to shift gears into the main channel. It runs fairly deep, with plenty of rock cover and a good population of 10 to 12 inch smallies.

From this point (38.41295,-77.64766) down to the end of the rocks and grass islands, there are a series of lakes to fish. Move to the right side, continuing to follow the main current, to where the river runs under a large overhanging tree. The center of the river is mostly sand with fewer rocks than exist on the right edge. The center stays up to three feet deep at summer lows.

38.41228,-77.64568 marks the downstream limit of the coverage in the book. As you stand on the final grass island and gaze downstream, realize you are 1.3 miles from your vehicle. Although you can see another grass section in the distance (downstream approximately a third of a mile), recognize that you have a long walk back to your vehicle. The quality of the river immediately in front of you is not encouraging. After overdosing on the rocks and grass in the last 300 feet, the river flips back to having a sandy, desert bottom. I'll leave it as an exercise for the reader to move farther downstream and discover what lies ahead.

This is the side channel that comprises the path to the downstream tip of the long island.

Looking downstream from the confluence of the side channel with the main river. It is deep and needs to be fished. The tall trees on the other side are the next target.

Do not be disappointed by the featureless view downstream. If you are willing to walk, there is good water (71 cfs).

Even though it is without visible features, plenty of rocks and ledges lie just under the surface. Look for ones close to dense shade.

The first line of rocks emerges.

Veer left to hit this large log.

This is a major landmark. There are good channels all around it.

Slide left to work the cuts leading to the shade.

The final rock garden.

When you stand at the tip of the last rock garden, there is another complex downstream.

Whew! Reset yourself back to the tip of the island.... If you do not want to head this far downstream, work over the good area immediately downstream of the junction and fish back to the campground in the main channel of the river. At the tip of the island, do not ignore the deep hole to the left of the confluence. Even if you already fished it on the way down, fish it again. When the water is clear, you can stand on the edge of the sandbar and see plenty of smallmouth and even a few catfish swimming alongside the submerged logs. Once done, move back to the center to continue upstream in the main channel - not the side channel on the west (your original path from the campsite).

Just short of a line of rocks that stretch across a river, there is a channel that splits the island and creates a miniature confluence where it joins the main flow of the river (38.416994,-77.65649). Fish the junction above and below the sandbar around the current seams. Given the flow of water and the food being carried by it, carefully fish up the left bank to the line of rocks. Once even with the line of rocks, pop up on them and walk to the right bank. There is good fishing underneath the trees and in the several deep channels that spin out from the right exit through the rapids.

Your mental attitude sours as you resume the hike upstream as a result of the sand that spreads out ahead of you. Do not despair. While the bottom retains plenty of sand, there are enough rocks and, in particular, grass beds along the left shore that provide adequate forage for smallmouth. If you blunder upstream without being cautious, you will be rewarded by the sight of large smallmouth scattering from the bank. The farther you move upriver, the shallower the water gets. Fish the left bank. At 38.41777,-77.65824, the river transitions from "ok" water to poor. Downstream is a mix of rocks and sand while upstream is mostly sand. Continue walking since you have to get back to the campground anyway and do not pause when you come to the fallen logs on the left bank at 38.41801,-77.65880. At wadeable water levels in the middle of summer, it is not worth fishing them since the sand collects around them - no depth. Instead, continue upstream to the next good water.

At 38.41844,-77.66047, there is a prominent grass island that splits the river, but the water remains uninteresting and shallow. 50 feet upstream at 38.418725,-77.662747, you can move back through the gap to return to the campground.

Looking left from the confluence at the tip of the island. Fish this spot carefully and thoroughly.

The water is calm upstream, but there are plenty of perpendicular ledges.

In the final leg into the gap leading to the campground, there is a decent lake.

Move through the gap on the left at this point to return to the campground.

Bottom Line

The Rappahannock River Campground is a superb fishing location. Either going upstream or downstream is a good choice. It basically comes down to whether you want to fish deep (go downstream) or rocks (go upstream).

Snake Castle Rock

Google Map Coordinates: 38.426221,-77.695507

Summary Rating

Parking	Red	Spin Fishing	Green
Canoe/Kayak Launch	Red	Fly Fishing	Green
Distance to River	Red	Smallmouth Structure	Green
Can Bike to River	Red	Wading Distance	Green
Physical Fitness	Red	Pressure	Green
Scenery	Green	Overall	Green

Beyond having the coolest name of any place on the Rappahannock, Snake Castle Rock is a superb fishing location. Ignore the downstream area and move immediately to the 3,000 feet of jagged rocks, large islands and deep water that awaits upstream. Early in the year when there is still plenty of water roaring towards Fredericksburg, expect to see plenty of kayakers and canoeists. Many stop at Snake Castle Rock to fish. If you want to guarantee a solitary experience, wait until mid-June when the water levels drop.

Getting to the Stream

North: The main road from the north is US 29/US 15. Follow this major highway south from Warrenton and turn left (east) on US 17. Turn right on VA 651 (Sumerduck Road). Turn left on VA 631 (Snake Castle Road) and follow it to the end.

South: From I-95, take exit 133B onto US 17 North (Warrenton Road). Follow US 17 for approximately 13 miles. Turn left on VA 651 (Sumerduck Road). Turn left on VA 631 (Snake Castle Road) and follow it to the end.

At the end of Snake Castle Road, City of Fredericksburg "posted" signs begin to populate the trees on the right edge of the road.

Unfortunately, there are no shoulders that would allow you to pull your vehicle out of the right-of-way prior to reaching the cul-de-sac. Drive all the way into the cul-de-sac and tuck your vehicle between the driveways to stay out of the way of the local residents.

Once you gear up, walk back up the road and look for the gap between the trees on the left (south) side at 38.43126,-77.69504. Do not get your hopes up when you see the nice trail that leads into the city property. Prepare for intense bushwhacking.

Follow the trail until it veers up into the private property on the right. In 2010, this point was marked by pink survey tape high on a tree. Turn left and follow the faint trail down the hill to link up with a dry streambed that guides you to the river. The streambed is oriented on a line that extends from 38.43126,-77.69504 to 38.42943,-77.69459 to 38.42764,-77.69448. In 2010, orange hunter's tape marked the first hundred yards of the dim trail. The trail eventually peters out, becoming indistinct as it blends into the thick vegetation that lines the bottom of the draw.

Use the dry streambed as the directional arrow to get the rest of the way to the river. Keep the streambed on the left and move in a southerly direction; weaving through thick brush and saplings. Eventually, the brush ends, abruptly transitioning onto an old dirt road. Follow the road to the left to the river.

Canoe/Kayak Comment: While some of the outfitters have access to Snake Castle to launch boats, you do not. Therefore, this is not the place to launch a canoe or kayak..

Environment and Fish

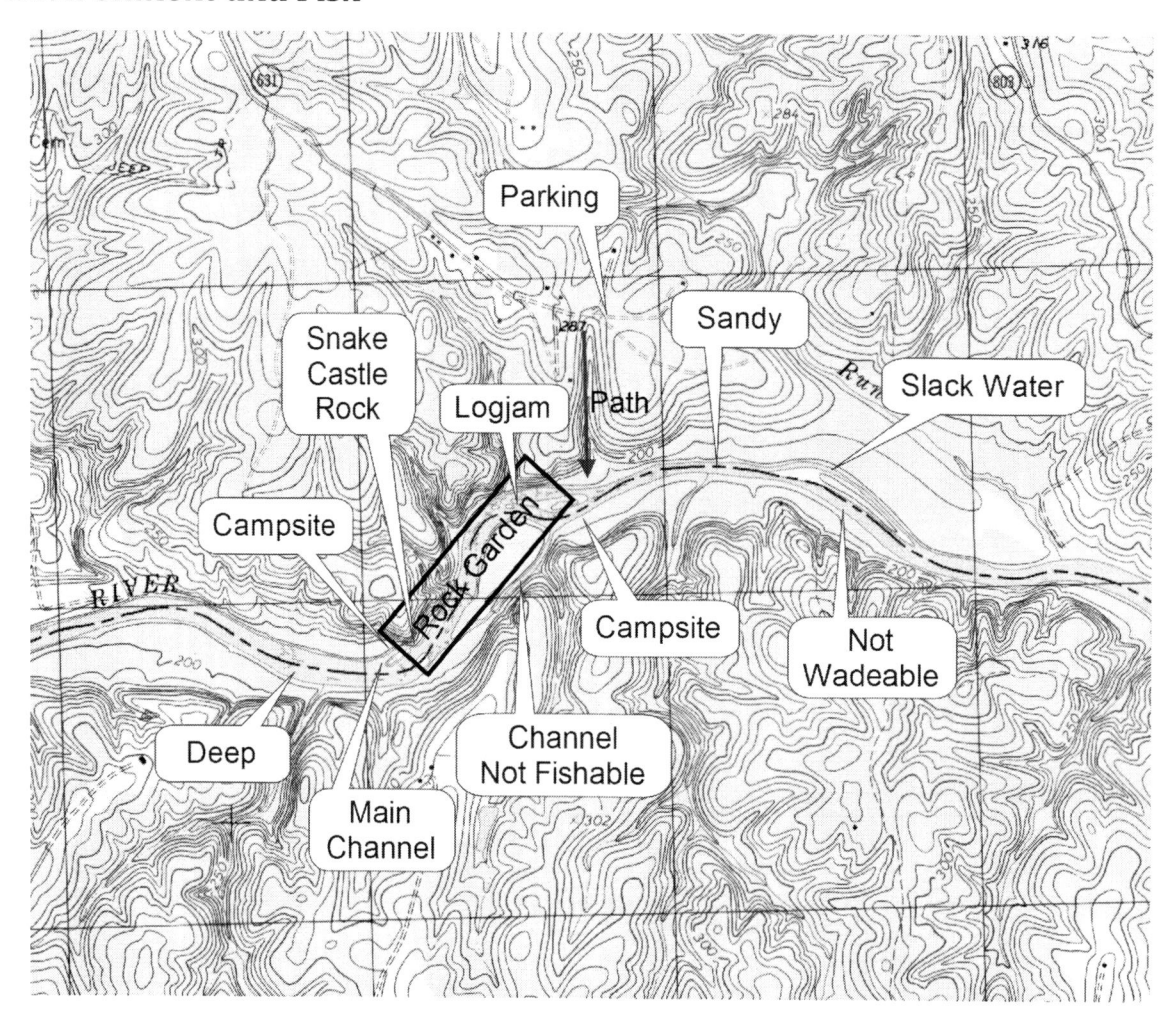

Classic smallmouth water greets you as you take the final sweaty steps to break out of the underbrush that squeezes tight to both sides of the old road. Upstream, there is a large logjam caught on a high rock surrounded by runs through grass islands. The downstream view is one of flat, wide water leading to a distant riffle. Adding interest to the scene is the downstream tip of the large island to the direct front where the river pools around a grass bed. Given a choice, upstream is a is the way to go.

Upstream

Sticking with the northern channel, there are three runs that charge downstream from the huge logjam (38.426009,-77.697217). Each run features pools deep enough to be interesting and all hold fish. My experience is that most of the smallmouth in these runs tend to be 12 inches and below. Use the pools as a warm-up, fishing each in turn as you move towards the logjam.

If you are not interested in warming up, the best channel is the one that runs next to the island. Move to the island bank and fish it to the logjam. Slide around the right side of the logjam to the deep pool upstream. If the water is running a little higher, the other two channels, fed by the flow around the right side of the logjam, might produce something, but they're usually too shallow.

Upstream of the logjam there are two main pushes of water. The minor one lies to the right and is directly upriver. The main, more interesting channel forces its way along the northern bank and is framed by a long sandbar with a grass island and scattered boulders.

Before moving any farther upstream, swing your eyes to the left to survey the flow running along the southern side of the island. There is a major ridge that reaches from the island to the sandbar (38.425662,-77.697274) on the shore creating significant pools on either side.

Fish the downstream pool. In addition to walking out on the tall rocks that provide the backbone to the ridge, move around the moon shaped sandbar on the northern border. You can easily spend 30 to 45 minutes fishing this 50 feet of ideal structure to catch as many sunfish and smaller bass as you want in the churn of water below the ridge. Begin to walk downstream along the southern bank of the island. There are two main runs that organize the water. The northern one is small, but productive (38.425618,-77.696567). Take a few throws and wade across to get closer to the southern shoreline to work the rocky structure that lies just under the surface of the water and shelters fish in small hiding holes. Continue downstream to the major gradient break at 38.42554,-77.695657.

In front of you is superb water. Do not be put off by either the small campsite on the southern shore or the glare of the brown sand where the water shallows out near the downstream tip of the island. This pool is where you will probably catch a trophy size smallmouth if you play your cards correctly. You will not be able to wade except along the shelf that extends from the perimeter. It is well worth clawing along either side to cover the 200 feet between the rocks and the tip of the island.

Walk back up to the logjam.

Fish the upstream side of the rock ridge that extends from the logjam and move upriver. There are two good channels feeding the ridge and both are deep enough to be worthwhile. Walk up the left side to target the next wide spot at 38.425629,-77.698086. This is a 30 foot wide circle whose boundaries are drawn by some tall rocks in the center of the river as well as the sandbar next to the shoreline. The circle divides into two distinct pools split down the middle by boulders. Move slowly as you approach the tail end of the large lake that is the next significant terrain feature and extends 100 feet upriver.

The northern side of the lake is uninteresting given the large, wide sandbar that stretches 30 feet out from the bank. On the other hand, the 60 feet of river bordering the southern shoreline remains densely rocky with an infinite number of pools that provide hiding locations for fish. Do not hurry through this section. Your best strategy is to fish up the center, staying to the left of the main current so you can fish the deep channel to the north. In the summer, the part of the river that borders the southern shoreline tends to get clogged with aquatic vegetation, which pushes you farther out towards the center. There are still plenty of fish that conceal themselves in the dense cover, but you will not be able to pull them out since there are few open holes providing a window through the weeds. The lake evaporates into tall boulders that segment the river in the vicinity of 38.424864,-77.6988.

The next 700 feet of river is all great fishing. There is nothing to distinguish any particular spot until you reach the dramatic rock structure at 38.423408,-77.699337. This area is teeming with runs, pools, boulders and congested vegetation to the left, and it is all infested with fish. If you caught a large fish near the campsite, this is where you will catch your next monster. Water conditions dictate the attack strategy. However, you cannot make a wrong decision – there is no bad way to fish through. The only thing I would caution is to stick with the current flows because that is where the food and the oxygen move downstream.

Once you climb up the dramatic boulders at the distant end, the river divides itself into two distinct ecosystems. The left edge, for the next 650 feet, is shallow with dense, large boulders preventing the penetration of a strong flow of water. They push the current to the northern bank. This is perfect. The edge of the boulder line becomes a catwalk to walk up the river and fish the deep section on the north. The first half of the lake is good smallmouth habitat. The lake starts out with a broken rocky bottom only to dissipate the closer you get to the actual Snake Castle Rock. The last 150 feet of the lake is sand. Normally, you would ignore it. Do not make that mistake here. Since the flow of the river is compressed as it runs around Snake Castle Rock just upstream, the sandy area represents the terminus of the major feeding channel. Continue to leverage the rocks on the left to move upstream and fish the channel all the way up to Snake Castle Rock at 38.421996,-77.701204.

Sadly, you are nearing the end of wadeable water. Other than the main channel, the area in the immediate vicinity of Snake Castle Rock is not fishable. The rocks push high enough above the river to limit penetration to small, shallow flows through narrow gaps. Walk onto the peninsula formed by a slim spit of land upstream of Snake Castle Rock. It is deep on either side. If you decide to fish the northern half first, that is where the current is strong and deep. The rocks lining the northern end of the peninsula are abrupt with few hand or toeholds. Be careful! For future reference, there is a campsite opposite the peninsula on the shore. Once done on the northern side, switch to the south.

While the river to the north runs quick and fast, it is slow to the south, offering the perception of being stagnant and uninteresting. Nothing could be further from the truth. Keep that deep running lure tied on because the water is equally deep. The advantage offered by the southern side is that there are two distinct ridgelines that run at a 45° angle from the peninsula giving you leverage to cast closer to the southern shore.

Fish back to the tall mix of large boulders that created the upstream boundary of Snake Castle. Even though this ends your upstream wading experience, you can console yourself that you get to fish back over the same 3,000 feet of prime water to reach the trail back to the road.

The massive logjam is at the center of this picture. Move to the left-hand bank.

This is the view downstream towards the tip of the island. This channel is not interesting.

The massive logjam is in the center of the picture and it shows the two best runs.

There is deep water above the logjam on the left-hand side at 72 cfs.

This is the broad lake that terminates in the wide sandbar on the right. Stay left.

Closer to Snake Castle Rock, the left bank becomes overgrown and stagnant at summer low levels.

To the left of snake Castle rock, there is one good channel (86 cfs).

This is Snake Castle Rock. Fish the very deep channel in front of it all the way downstream to the end.

This is the "stagnant" side of the island upstream from the rock.

This is the main channel of the river that leads into the rock.

The view from the tip of the island reveals a broad lake that is not wadeable.

Once you walk back down to the entry point, move to the other side of the first large island to hit the deep water.

Snake Castle Rock   103

On the other side of the island, the campsite is near the last gradient break.

Upstream from the campsite, there are several good channels that all hold fish.

After the gradient break, the river creates a good lake immediately in front of the campsite. Work around the edges to pick up a large fish.

Another view into the opposite side of the island from the upstream tip.

Downstream

If you decide to go downstream, swing back upstream at the tip of the island to fish the good water that extends 200 feet from the tip, past the campsite, to the first rapid. It is important that you do that since fishing there will be the only good fishing you will experience once you start your downstream trek. Actually, the first 250 feet downstream from the center island is okay – barely. You have the typical underwater rock structure that leads up to a small outcropping of rock at 38.426709,-77.69236. If you squint at the broad expanse of water downstream, you may fall victim to angler's excitement over all the new territory and the implied promise of fish. In particular, since you will not see anyone else fishing downstream even if there are other people in the Snake Castle complex, you might be anxious to have a more solitary experience. You will – because there will not be any fish there either. The lake covers a barren, sandy bottom.

Immediately after the rocky outcropping, the river becomes grossly shallow and sandy. Even at a gage height of 2.412 feet at Fredericksburg, the river is merely inches deep with a few random one to two foot sections in various spots. In the distance, grass islands interspersed with tall rocks hint of better water. It is a quick walk in the shallow water to move the half mile to the head of the small set of riffles that looked much better from a distance than they do up close. The tall sand dune on the left creates a major terrain feature that is a perfect observation platform. Climb to the top of the small hill (38.42679,-77.68732) and survey the dismal scene.

On the left is a small trickle of water dribbling down the north side of the 200 foot wide island that extends 2, 000 feet downstream. To the right is the main channel with the majority of the flow. Neither is any good since they only provide a place for the slowing current to dump sand as the energy ebbs after the river exhausts itself in Snake Castle.

Since you are here anyway, you may as well fish the deep water at the base of the riffle. You have approximately 40 feet of good water with rocks where the main flow of the current gained a little momentum with the elevation drop and scoured the bottom clean. Do not bother to fish beyond the small break that separates the hill from the main island. The river deepens and is unwadeable. Even if it was, there is nothing compelling to make either you or fish hang out farther downstream.

The early morning glare hides how bad downstream will be.

Farther downstream, the river disintegrates into a mix of sand and scattered grass at 86 cfs.

Sandbars predominate as you trudge downriver.

You may be able to start to pick up a few fish in the deep water in the middle.

This is the view upstream from the tall hill. If you come this far down, fish underneath the trees on the left-hand bank.

The hill creates a brief moment of fast water as the river compresses to move through the gap, making the spot immediately downstream fishable.

Bottom Line

Ignore the downstream section and focus upstream. With your first step upriver, you move into a 3,000 foot long angler's paradise on par with the Confluence.

Phelps Wildlife Management Area

The 4,539 acre Phelps Wildlife Management Area (WMA) offers seven miles of fishing along the river and includes the popular put-in for kayaks and canoes at Kellys Ford.

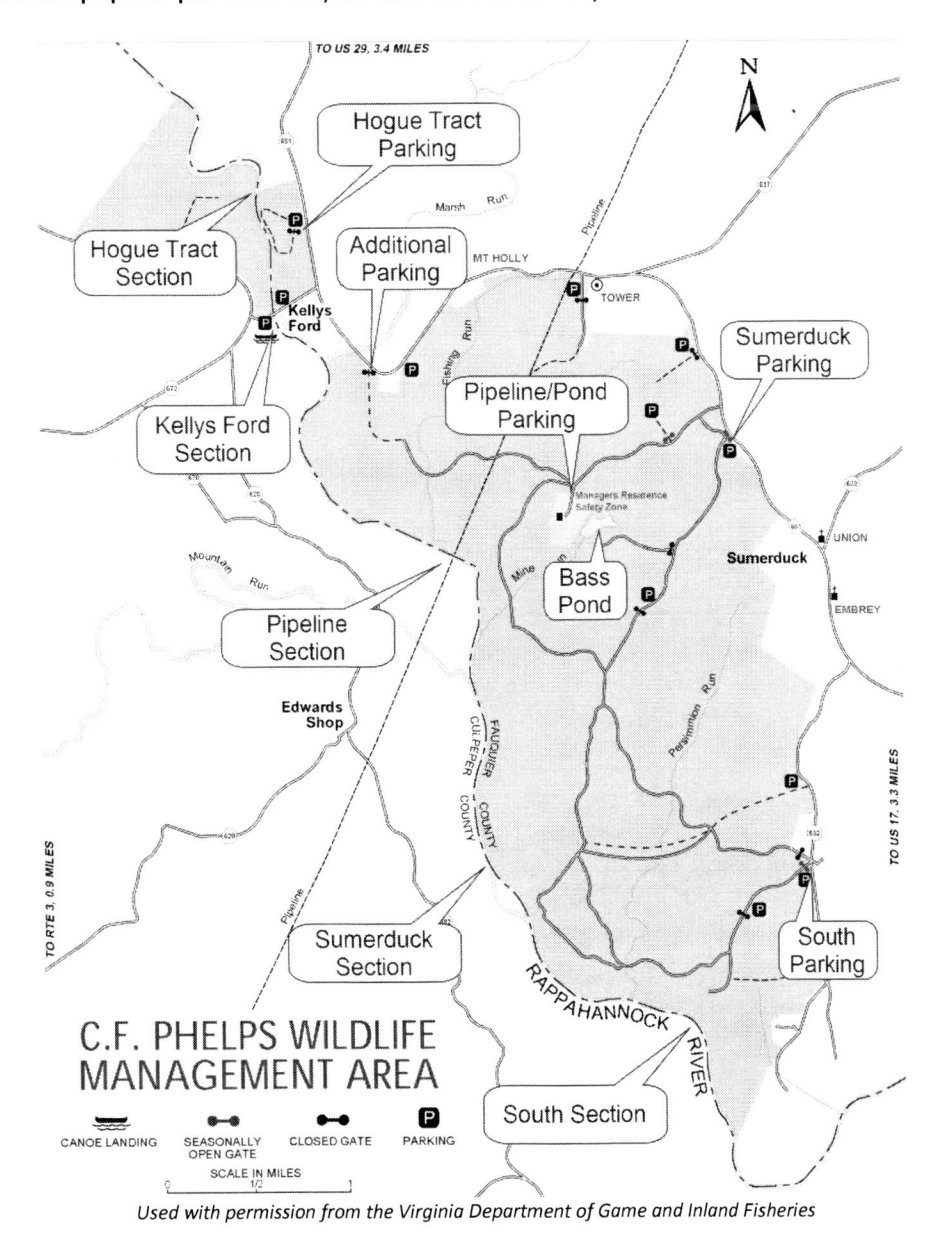

Used with permission from the Virginia Department of Game and Inland Fisheries

Phelps WMA South

Google Map Coordinates: 38.425933,-77.742101

Summary Rating

Parking	Green	Spin Fishing	Green
Canoe/Kayak Launch	Red	Fly Fishing	Green
Distance to River	Red	Smallmouth Structure	Yellow
Can Bike to River	Green	Wading Distance	Green
Physical Fitness	Red	Pressure	Green
Scenery	Yellow	Overall	Green

The southern access point is the best spot in the WMA to fish below Kellys Ford. Even then, do not expect to encounter spectacular, classic bass water. With few exceptions, most of the river upstream from Snake Castle Rock slowly flows over a sandy bottom.

Getting to the Stream

North: From I-66, take exit 43A onto US 29 South at Gainesville. Follow US 29 for 19 miles and turn south on US 17. Follow it for just under 11 miles. Turn right on VA 634 (Courtneys Corner Road) followed by a left onto VA 615 (South River Road). After 0.5 miles, take the first right onto VA 632 (Union Church Road) and follow it for three miles to turn left on VA 651 (Sumerduck Road). Continue for just over 0.5 miles and turn right on VA 632 (Rogers Ford Road). Follow it south for 1.5 miles until reaching the marked parking area on the right at 38.436212,-77.729323.

South: Follow US 29 north from Culpeper to turn right onto Kellys Ford Road (VA 674) prior to crossing the Rappahannock at Remington. Follow Kellys Ford Road for five miles and turn left on VA 620 (Edwards Shop Road). After a short distance, turn right on VA 651 (Sumerduck Road). Continue on Sumerduck for 4.5 miles and turn right on VA 632 (Rogers Ford Road). Follow Rogers Ford south for 1.5 miles until reaching the marked parking area on the right at 38.436212,-77.729323.

Getting to the parking lot is only the first challenge. It is an easy one mile walk to reach the river. If you use a bike, you can ride it most of the way but there is one tricky spot.

Follow the road past the locked gate and ignore the turn to the shooting range on the right at 38.432288,-77.736089. During hunting season, the VDGIF opens the upper gate and allows vehicular traffic to the parking area next to the range. Continue south on the road for another 450 feet until reaching a clearing (38.430171,-77.736824). The road continues south to the left along the treeline that parallels a field.

Do not follow that road. Instead, cut across the clearing and look for a small brown sign that warns horses against using the slight trail.

Immediately behind that sign, through the dense brush, is the narrow trail that leads down the steep hill to the open field next to the river. Lock your bike to a tree and walk the rest of the way.

The river bank is steep and high. Do not walk downriver on the northern bank because there is no easy access to the river moving in that direction. In addition, you would spook the fish in the superb section that extends 200 yards downstream from the entry point. Walk along the shoreline until you see the well beaten cut that leads down to the river. There are actually two of them. Pick either one, slide down and hop into the river. I prefer the one at 38.42582,-77.74169. Both are muddy and slick after a rain.

Canoe/Kayak Comment: The long walk from the parking area eliminates this as a potential put-in or a take-out.

Environment and Fish

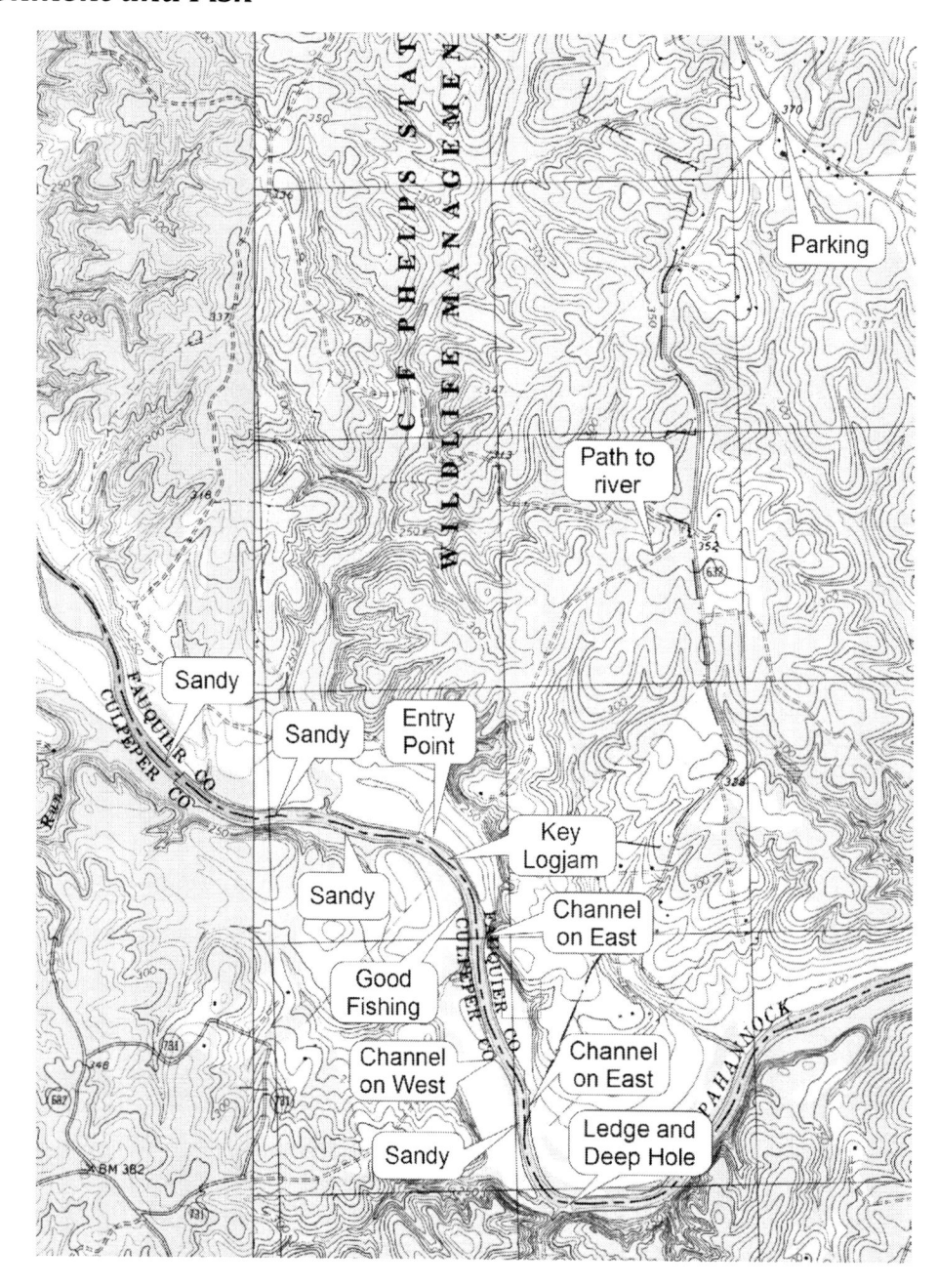

The Rappahannock continues its trend of providing good and bad choices. In this case, pointing your rod upstream results in a wasted day while moving down provides the exact opposite. This entire section is mostly sand, but includes enough depth and fallen structure along the downriver shoreline to hold exceptionally good fish.

Upstream

As you stand in the shallow riverbed next to a set of scattered rocks, it all looks good. The slick glare off the top of the river upstream hides the disaster that lies in front of you. The river slows as it runs next to the southern boundary of the wildlife management area, spreading out to between 50 and 75 feet wide and losing velocity as it extends over the additional surface area. No velocity means that sand and silt are not propelled downstream and are left to accumulate across the broad expanse of the river.

You cannot help but notice the sand. At summer levels, the water might hit the top of your wading boots. If you insist on moving upstream, be prepared to catch sunfish and a random, confused bass that is desperately seeking better water. There are no landmarks to guide the trip. While the northern shoreline has the "deepest" channel, it is not deep enough to be interesting to anything significant. It seems as if the majority of the fallen structure also lies on the northern bank and you can exploit it as you walk upstream.

There is a power line that runs across the river at 38.426611,-77.750283 and even it does not offer up the normal productive water. Upstream from the power line, the river turns into a bend where there is some better water on the southern bank, but nothing to brag about and certainly not worth the effort to get there. The power line is 2,500 feet away from the gash in the shoreline that allowed you to step into the river.

Beyond the power line, the river takes a gradual turn to the north. By this time, you will be anxious and wondering how the river can go so long without a ledge, a line of rocks or even a riffle. All that greets you as you stagger north is a continued wet, sandy, desolate tract. If you are willing to walk another 1,500 feet upstream, you finally encounter a small rocky section (38.429246,-77.754912) where Mill Run and Hoopers Run join the river from the left. The rocky area extends approximately 150 feet upstream and, in the end, is not worth the sweat. Besides, you are 0.91 miles from where you slid into the river and almost two miles away from your vehicle. This section is so bad that it was not worth taking many pictures. Here are two representative shots that tell the story.

Even though this looks good, do not even think about fishing upstream at 46 cfs.

The glare off the water hides the shallows. Nothing but sand!

Downstream

Downstream is the exact opposite of upstream. Even though the river maintains its sandy bottom all the way down to the major riffle at 38.412876,-77.734458, there is enough depth and associated structure to provide exceptionally good fishing.

Walk a short distance downriver until you see a cluster of fallen trees on the left side (38.425348,-77.740335). There is a crescent shaped sandbar that runs from north to south and parallels the southern bank downstream. That spot marks the first location in what will be 200 yards of good water. The majority of the current moves quickly along the northern bank. Fish the current seam where it begins to slide down the right side of the log structure. Initially, the river is shallow, but deepens to over 10 feet at the middle of the logjam. You can stand in that single spot and fish for an hour. Use top water lures along the edge of the logs and then switch to deep running baits that get all the way to the bottom.

Slowly fish down the log until the river begins to shallow out again. The sandbar continues along the southern shore and provides the highway downriver. Continue to concentrate on the northern bank. The deep channel persists with the next interesting structure being two fallen logs that lay parallel to the direction of flow at 38.425019,-77.739962. In addition to smallmouth bass, there are some huge fallfish that love this particular spot. Fish on either side of the logs and be prepared to haul hard if something hits between the logs and the shore. If using fly gear, use a minimum of 4x tippet so you can apply strong pressure to keep the fish from wrapping around the logs.

The channel below the two logs shallows out and becomes mostly sand for the next 400 feet. At 38.424175,-77.739393, rocks reappear with a grass bed along the left bank. At the bend, the deep section jumps from east to west and it will be unwadeable on that side into the bend. Stay on the sandbar to fish both banks with an intense focus to the west. Beyond that, the good channel continues on the left bank down to the minor riffle at 38.422237,-77.738944. Spend a decent amount of time fishing the section upstream where the water pools as well as the 40 feet of good rocky structure on the left bank below the rock line. The best path forward is on a sand hump in the center.

While you can continue to fish downstream, the next 1,500 feet will not be as good as what you experienced between your entry point and the riffle. To keep from getting bored as you slosh south, fish the good, shaded structure on the eastern shore. There are scattered rocks, fallen logs and sometimes thick underwater vegetation that provides habitat for some 12 inch smallmouth - they will keep you entertained through the next bend.

At 38.416902,-77.736965, the river takes a slight turn to the south with the next 300 feet being pretty good water. What attracts fish is the long, stringy tendrils of underwater vegetation that wrap tightly around the rocks. Even at the height of summer, the vegetation is not oppressive. Clearly, the bass enjoy all the opportunities to hide offered by the underwater cover. Amazingly, the right bank continues to be uninteresting.

Once the river transitions back to sand, walk directly down to the final bend at 38.412989,-77.735359 to work over a gradient break created by the dramatic change in direction. The river boils around a peninsula that extends from the southern bank where it compresses the flow and increases the velocity. The scouring effect scrubs the bottom clean and exposes plenty of good rocks. Beyond that point, the river returns to being mostly sand, shallow and boring. Head back upstream.

Fish this logjam aggressively. It is the first one you encounter after you start moving downstream.

You can pick up a couple of nice fish like this if you work the log carefully.

This is the overall view looking downstream once you enter the river. The good bank is on the left – ignore the right-hand bank.

Halfway to the turn and the left bank continues to be good at 46 cfs.

This is the small gradient break and grass island next to the gazebo on the left-hand bank. Be sure to hit the good spot to the left on the other side of the grass bank.

Downstream from the turnaround point is flat and returns to sand. If you have the energy, continue to fish downstream until you hit the sand line.

Bottom Line

Downriver, downriver, downriver! Definitely do not waste time fishing upstream from the entry. You can have a great day fishing the first 200 yards downriver and that makes the one mile walk worthwhile.

Phelps WMA Sumerduck

Google Map Coordinates: 38.468363,-77.736751

Summary Rating

Parking	Green	Spin Fishing	Green
Canoe/Kayak Launch	Red	Fly Fishing	Green
Distance to River	Red	Smallmouth Structure	Red
Can Bike to River	Green	Wading Distance	Green
Physical Fitness	Red	Pressure	Green
Scenery	Yellow	Overall	Red

If you enjoy riding a bike or taking a long hike, that is the only pleasure gained from fishing this location. There is one good spot upstream, downstream is a waste of time. Reminder! The "Green" ratings for spin and fly fishing only indicate that you can use that type of gear without restriction, and does not imply that a place is good.

Getting to the Stream

North: From Warrenton, take US 29/15 south. Turn left on US 17 and follow it to turn right on VA 637 (Shipps Store Road). VA 637 merges with VA 634 (Courtney's Corner Road). Continue on VA 634 through its intersection with VA 651 (Sumerduck Road). Turn left and follow VA 651 for about a mile. The parking area is on the right (38.468363,-77.736751).

South: From Culpeper, drive north on VA 29/15. Turn right on VA 674 (Kellys Ford Road). Turn left on VA 620 (Edwards Shop Road) to go across the river and make an immediate right on VA 651 (Sumerduck Road). Proceed on VA 651 for just over three miles. The parking area is on the right (38.468363,-77.736751).

Approximately 500 feet before the Sumerduck parking area, there is another dirt road extending off to the west. It is framed by two white brick pillars. Use that as a "heads up" warning that the Sumerduck is close. Just to complete the description, there is a road that leads to this same area from the Phelps WMA South access point. I have not personally hiked or biked it since the fishing was not good enough to merit multiple trips.

Canoe/Kayak Comment: The distance to the river rules this out as a potential launch point.

Environment and Fish

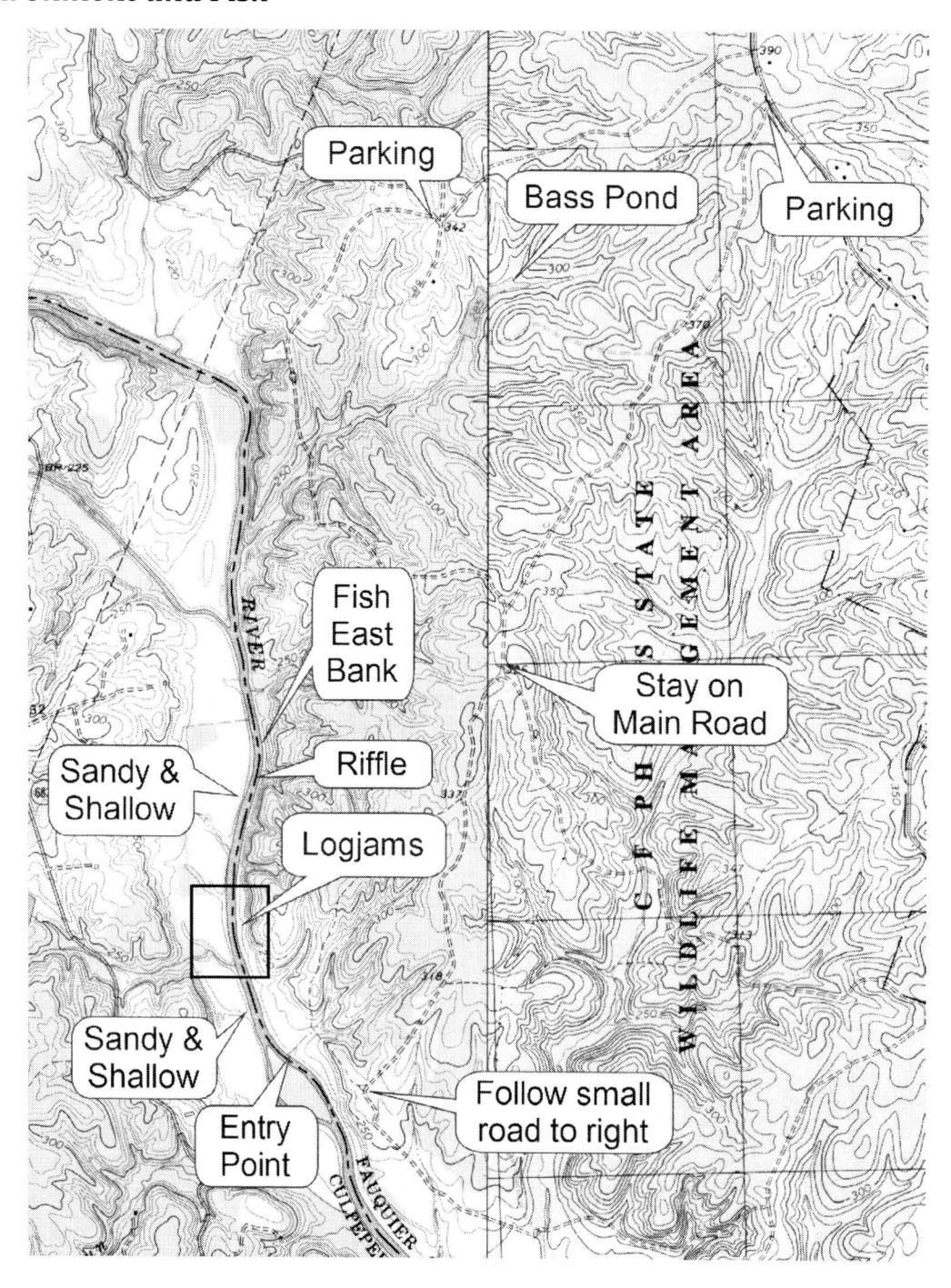

This access point is the most physically demanding on the Rappahannock. The river is 3.25 miles away from the parking area depending on the season. During hunting season, the upper gate is open and you can drive an additional mile down the dirt road to reach the parking lot at the center of the wildlife management area (38.45602,-77.74471).

The best way to get to the river is not to walk, but to ride a bike. Even during hunting season, when the last gate is open, you still are looking at 2.25 miles to get to the river and the same distance to return to your vehicle.

A good mountain bike allows you to coast most of the way since the road drops 341 feet in elevation between the upper parking lot and the river. Use a section of PVC pipe to hold your rod.

There is one confusing turn after the hunting season parking lot at 38.43785,-77.75203. The main body of the road runs to the left with the right fork transitioning from hard packed dirt and gravel to mostly grass. You need to be alert because it is easy to continue on the left fork since it is the larger road, but the grassy right fork leads to the river. With all of the large, loose gravel, even this road becomes a little bit difficult since bike tires may tend to spin in the loose gravel as you scramble up some of the gentle hills. The road leads through an open field and eventually comes to a "T" intersection. Turn right and continue on the road for another thousand feet looking for a left turn at approximately 38.43549,-77.75833. At this point, the road disappears into a muddy trail leading into a 20 yard wide beaten area. If you did not know the river was nearby, you would assume you are still in the middle of the woods. Park your bike and walk 50 feet south through dense underbrush to reach the river.

In the previous chapter, I discussed the upstream section from the Phelps WMA South access point. That discussion ended just below this spot, so I will only describe the water upstream.

The bank is steep, so carefully pick your spot to slide down - since you are over three miles from your vehicle, this is no place to have an accident. Mark the exit point because everything looks the same from the river. Unless it is swept away in a future flood, there is a large log pushed up against the bank near where you emerge from the woods. Make a mental note of that spot or leave a more visible signal to yourself on the side of the bank so you know where to climb out at the end of the day. The last thing you want to happen is to miss the exit point on the way back out, if you do, you will have to bushwhack through a considerable amount of underbrush to get back to the main road. Besides, you do not want to lose track of your bike.

Once on the river, it doesn't look all that good. At summer lows, the Rappahannock barely moves. Walk upstream to the tip of the island that divides the river into two channels. The water to the right is the main flow. It is not worth fishing down the channel on the opposite side of the island since there is not enough current pushing on that side to make it an attractive holding area for smallmouth. During higher water conditions, that could change and you can make the call when you put your eyes on it.

As you stand on the tip and look upstream, the brown sheen of a broad desert spreads annoyingly into the distance. The river bottom is totally unattractive for smallmouth and is unvaryingly sandy. But, since you just pedaled or walked 3.25 miles to get here, move upstream to fish the one very good spot in this section. Given the sandy nature of the bottom, you should not have great expectations for finding a significant number of smallmouth in the vicinity of the island. Start walking upstream and, if you feel you must, fish the deeper water that squeezes in a narrow channel against the right bank. There are a number of blowdowns and log clusters to target. Even at summer lows, the sandy "lake" stays between two and three feet deep. It is easy wading up the center and the depth at the edge provides a limited amount of protection and habitat for fish.

The only reason to move upstream is to fish a single, solitary location. There are two significant landmarks approximately 0.4 miles upstream at 38.43973,-77.76173. Both are prominent tangles of logs. Approach cautiously, because this is the only compelling structure in the entire stretch. As you near the logjam, notice the extended sandbar stretching downstream from the jam on the right. This is the clue that the main channel of the river now pushes against the left bank. Before reaching the deep area in the immediate vicinity of the jams, move to the left bank before it gets too deep to fish the downstream end of the left logjam. Throw to the base and work around the outside. If the water is clear, you will be surprised to see a number of boulders scattered around the perimeter. Their presence, along with the fallen trees, is what combines with the depth to make this an attractive and compelling spot. Slowly work to the right, continuing to throw towards the fallen tree. Expand your attack to include the center channel since there are even more boulders buried in the deep water. In fact, it is so deep, you will not be able to wade beyond this point unless you move to the right bank.

As you swing around to the right, move toward the other logjam on the right bank. Begin to throw next to it, working out towards the center of the river. There is a dense bed of vegetation growing on the outside edge that extends into the river for approximately five feet. Therefore, cast at least that far from the log to ensure the lure bumps the bottom on the outside edge of the bed to coax hiding fish into striking. Depending on the water levels, this may be the end of your wading trip. If you decide you want to go farther upstream, you need to exit the river and walk along the right bank (the left bank is private property) or skinny along the outside edge of the right log. The good, deep water ends 50 yards upstream of the logjam at 38.44070,-77.76177.

If there ever was truth to the saying that 90% of the fish live in 10% of the water, it is true here and, as you walk farther upstream, you head away from where the 90% live. In fact, I recommend against any farther progress upstream. It is simply not worth the effort. But, if you are compelled to discover new water, gradually move towards the left bank since the right is where the current flows. If you are looking for something to throw at, there is a root ball supporting an overhanging tree on the right that marks the location of a small deep spot.

In addition to being slightly deeper than the center of the river, the right bank features an explosive growth of underwater vegetation that holds fingerlings. Therefore, you may actually run into some significant fish if you happen to luck onto the grass beds during the prime feeding times in the morning or the evening and catch the big boys "on patrol."

At 38.44266,-77.76150, the river briefly begins to support a mix of flat rock and sand on the bottom and false optimism may return, thinking that the structure of the river is going to change for the better. Unfortunately, even though there are a few rocky bumps poking above the surface of the water, it remains shallow. The riffle in the distance marks the one mile point from where you entered the river. While there is nothing compelling to fish in the vicinity of the riffle, your eyes might gravitate to the shore and notice a picnic table the landowner positioned on the high bluff overlooking the river. In many cases, a minor landmark like this indicates that there could be good fishing - after all, why bother otherwise? Unfortunately, it is just a pretty place to have a picnic. Upstream of the table, the deep channel runs next to the right bank where the thick grass beds swirl out approximately 20 feet into the river. Since you are here anyway, walk onto the shallow shelf that extends from the left bank to get within casting range and work the grass beds upstream for the next 50 yards.

Since you are over a mile from your entry point, this is a good place to turn around and walk back for two reasons. First, it is a mile from the entry point. Second, there is nothing interesting upstream. If you were to continue upstream for another quarter mile, all you would do is walk through a sandy desert that gets shallower and shallower. A better idea is to walk downstream to the dual logjam and fish them for another hour on the way back out.

Mentally mark to the fallen log on the right-hand side. It is the landmark indicating the place to leave the river to return to the road.

Once you walk to the tip of the island, it is a disappointing view that extends into the distance – sand! (32 cfs)

Wade upstream until you see this logjam on the right.

And this one on the left.

Close to the bend, the river has some marginal rock structure on the right-hand side as it goes into the corner.

Beyond the corner, although you can see some rocks in the distance, it is not worth walking up to fish them.

Bottom Line

A long ride or hike leads to marginal water that only has one good location to fish.

Phelps WMA Middle (Pipeline)

Google Map Coordinates: 38.464789,-77.752037

Summary Rating

Parking	Green	Spin Fishing	Green
Canoe/Kayak Launch	Red	Fly Fishing	Green
Distance to River	Red	Smallmouth Structure	Red
Can Bike to River	Green	Wading Distance	Green
Physical Fitness	Red	Pressure	Green
Scenery	Yellow	Overall	Yellow

This is another one dimensional location. Ignore upstream unless you need exercise. Walk as far as you can downstream to enjoy the better fishing.

Getting to the Stream

North: From Warrenton, take US 29/15 south. Turn left on US 17 and follow it to turn right on VA 637 (Shipps Store Road). VA 637 merges with VA 634 (Courtney's Corner Road). Continue on VA 634 through its intersection with VA 651 (Sumerduck Road). Turn left and follow VA 651 for about a mile.

South: From Culpeper, drive north on VA 29/15. Turn right on VA 674 (Kellys Ford Road). Turn left on VA 620 (Edwards Shop Road) to go across the river and make an immediate right on VA 651 (Sumerduck Road). Proceed on VA 651 for just over three miles.

Make a right turn onto the gravel road framed by two white brick pillars. Follow it for approximately 0.75 miles and take the left fork. There is a small sign on the right warning that further vehicular travel on the right fork is prohibited. Stay to the left and you will see a small kiosk in the distance. You may park anywhere between the fork and the kiosk. Do not to drive all the way to the kiosk because you will just end up walking back to the fork to follow it to the river. Therefore, park at the upper end of the lot as close to the intersection (38.464789,-77.752037) as you can.

Walk down the hard packed dirt road and resist the temptation to turn left on the grass road extending south towards the river at 38.462337,-77.757134 approximately 0.4 miles from the parking. It loops back to the parking area and does not get close to the river. Persevere on the main road until it intersects the pipeline easement at 38.46169,-77.761919. The walking is easy and the road is relatively level with only one small uphill pitch to negotiate on the way back. From the intersection of the road and the easement, it is a short 0.17 miles south to the river with the total distance from the parking area being 0.9 miles. At the edge of the river, move to the left side of the easement for the best path down the steep bank.

Follow the road to the right. It is easy walking or even better bike riding.

When you hit the pipeline easement, cut left and walk to the river.

Canoe/Kayak Comment: The long hike or bike from the parking area completely eliminates this as a potential launch point.

If you did drag it to the river, you still have to negotiate the steep bank.

The best way to enter the river is on the east side.

Environment and Fish

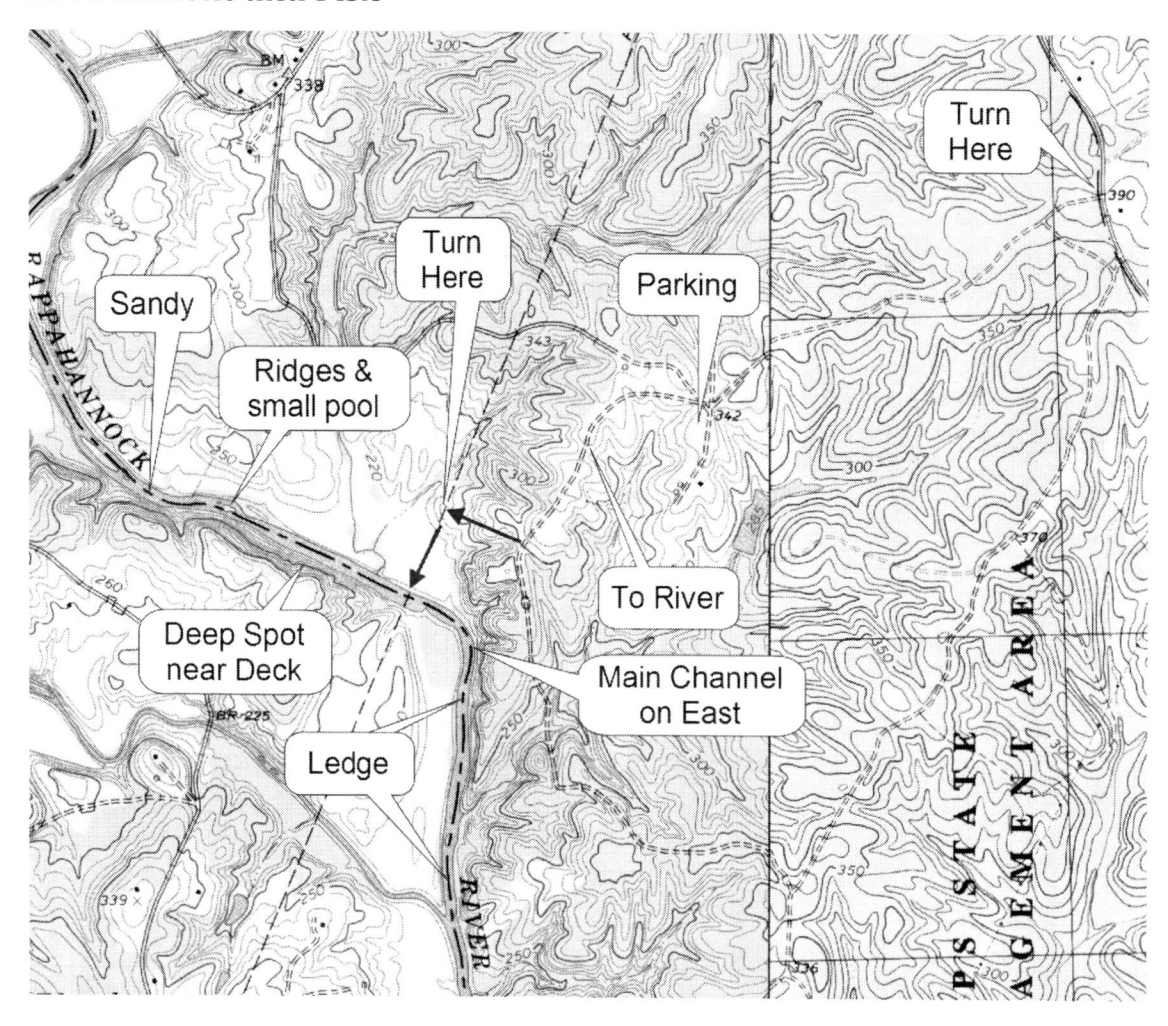

[Map showing Rappahannock River with labels: Turn Here, Sandy, Turn Here, Parking, Ridges & small pool, To River, Deep Spot near Deck, Main Channel on East, Ledge, and STATE MANAGEMENT AREA]

This far upriver, you cannot expect a significant amount of velocity. The bottom structure reflects that characteristic and is mostly sand with widely dispersed rock ridges.

Upstream

As you stand in the middle of the river after sliding down the precipitous bank, look in both directions. The instant conclusion is that downstream is the better direction to go based on the structure that lines the left bank, which was created and is constantly massaged by the flow of the compressed current. Upstream, the river is wide and appears to be extremely shallow with a pathetic brown color, hinting of a barren desert, shining through the shallow water. Since you are an angler, by default, you are also an optimist and are instantly drawn to the tortured logjam 0.1 miles upriver at 38.46036,-77.76578. The logical, optimistic assumption is that it breaks the flow of the river, causing the water to carve out a deep hole underneath it. Good call. Unfortunately, that is the only fishable spot in the initial stretch. Smallmouth loiter there during the heat of the day when they can take advantage of the shade provided by the shoreline vegetation and the collected moss that decorates the branches.

Pick up a fish or two and then back to reality. You are still in the middle of a dead zone with a flat sand bottom. But, since you have come this far, you may as well continue to walk upriver. The next landmark is a dramatic deck the landowner built just downstream of a sheer rock face that protrudes into the river (38.46063,-77.76692). Quickly admire the construction and then get back to fishing. Just upstream of the deck, the left bank becomes rocky with the pool in front of the cliff being at least five feet deep. If you sneak up on the spot when the water is clear, you can sight-fish for the large smallmouth that hang near the bottom. The fishing is pretty good for the 25 yards upstream from the deck.

Continue to ignore the right bank - it is pure sand with no interesting habitat for either fish or fishermen. At the end of the cliff, you are 0.33 miles from the pipeline easement and are within sight of more promising water upstream at the bend. There is nothing appealing until you get there and you should use the highway provided by the large sandbar in the middle of the river to avoid having to slog through the six inch deep water.

Your perseverance will be rewarded with a small pool that spins out below the top of the "S" turn created where the river runs through a major network of rock ridges (38.461723,-77.769503). Farther upstream, the river carves a deep channel on the left edge (38.462004,-77.771318) where it runs over a mix of small rocks and gravel. It obtains enough depth where it backs up between some ribbons of rock that run at a 45° angle to hold smallmouth. Do not rush; spend time here. In fact, if you waste a lot of time downstream, you will regret it. Continue to fish up the left edge, particularly next to the bank. The entire bottom between this location and the sand island (38.463546,-77.775013) in the distance is decent smallmouth country. It will be better earlier in the year when there is more water.

Above the small window of good bottom structure, the river returns to a mix of sand and mud. This is where you should turn around. Doing the math, you are 0.6 miles from the pipeline easement and over 1.5 miles from your vehicle.

The net of moving upstream from the easement is that it is not really worth it. As you head upstream, you spend more time hiking through shin deep water to get to a few marginally attractive spots than fishing.

Target the tangled trees to the right front. Move from there to hit the shoreline on the left bank.

Look for this dramatic deck and fish the good water just upstream.

Beyond the area near the deck, the water becomes boring at 34 cfs. Use the broad sandbar as your pathway upriver.

Once you find the small hole below a gradient break on the left, fish it and return.

Downstream

Even though the river runs across a shallow shelf at the easement, the downstream view is much more pleasing than upstream. Since the 0.9 mile walk to the river's edge put the appropriate amount of distance between you and any perception of pressure, begin fishing right away. Move to the middle of the river and fish the superb structure that hugs the left bank. The main channel bumps into the left bank with a gentle, lazy pressure. However, there is enough energy to carve out three and four foot deep holes near the log structure. Even at the height of summer when the river is low, this is where you will pick up some good bass.

Farther downstream, approach the line of rocks cautiously (38.45696,-77.76125). While the right bank has been primarily sand up to this point, a compact nest of solid rock structure with deep cuts and ridges lies just on the other side of the line of rocks. Sneak up and fish downstream into it. After you work the right and center, be sure to fish the grass bed that stretches all the way down to the left. The best tactic is to approach on the right side, fishing the center on the way down and the grass bank on the way back. 38.45696,-77.76125 is 1.5 miles from the parking area.

The rock island extends from the left bank and signals a shift in the bottom from being solid rock ledges to gravel and cobble with more sand on the right while maintaining smaller rock ledges on the left. This continues down the left bank for 25 yards downstream and makes it the ideal place to slow down and fish hard with both top water and subsurface patterns. Cast them underneath the overhanging trees. Bounce them over and through the cracks and crevices of the ridges. It is safe to ignore the right bank since it is the sandy side.

The river has settled into a consistent pattern of shallow rocky shelves on the left and sand on the right. Fish downstream as far as you have the energy to penetrate and look for the deeper holes between the ridges that run at a 45° angle across the river. The next significant landmark is a single rock in the middle of the river. The rock marks the end of the deep channel on the left side. It is certainly worth fishing in front of it and along the long blowdown on the left bank just behind it. Be sure to go weedless near the large blowdown because a substantial amount of grass grows approximately 20 feet into the river from the logs. If you do not have a GPS with you, just look for the cleared area on the right bank where the landowner plopped a picnic table overlooking the river. Not only is it good to know that there is civilization close by in case you get into trouble, but this also marks the place you should turn around.

Your first impression downstream is favorable. The current picks up and runs quickly.

Skip the sand and walk directly to where the first line of rocks appears (34 cfs).

There is a deep rocky channel underneath the root ball of this tree. If you find places like this, they will be the most productive.

Do not be tricked by the brown color that glares up through the water. There are plenty of rocky ledges that have been coated with dirt, but this is where the fish hang out.

There is a substantial amount of underwater vegetation, along with rocks, in this spot.

When you see the picnic table, turn around and head back.

Bottom Line

If you want to experience the best of both directions, fish the logs immediately upstream of the easement and then turn around and move as far downstream as you have the energy to go. While upstream is mostly sand, downstream features a balanced mix of rocks and vegetation surrounded by sand.

Phelps WMA Bass Pond

Google Map Coordinates: 38.463849,-77.752091

Summary Rating

Parking	Green	Spin Fishing	Green
Canoe/Kayak Launch	Yellow	Fly Fishing	Yellow
Distance to River	Green	Smallmouth Structure	Red
Can Bike to River	Red	Wading Distance	Red
Physical Fitness	Green	Pressure	Yellow
Scenery	Yellow	Overall	Red

The bass pond is worth a few minutes if you are here to fish the pipeline access, but is not a destination location for a full day of sport. The pond is only 200 yards from the parking area, is surrounded by parkland with benches, and is a pleasant place to spend some time.

Getting to the Pond

North: From Warrenton, take US 29/15 south. Turn left on US 17 and follow it to turn right on VA 637 (Shipps Store Road). VA 637 merges with VA 634 (Courtney's Corner Road). Continue on VA 634 through its intersection with VA 651 (Sumerduck Road). Turn left and follow VA 651 for about a mile.

South: From Culpeper, drive north on VA 29/15. Turn right on VA 674 (Kellys Ford Road). Turn left on VA 620 (Edwards Shop Road) to go across the river and make an immediate right on VA 651 (Sumerduck Road). Proceed on VA 651 for just over three miles.

Make a right turn onto the gravel road framed by two white brick pillars. Follow it for approximately 0.75 miles and take the left hand fork. There is a small sign on the right warning that further vehicular travel is prohibited. Stay to the left and you will see a small kiosk in the distance. Drive down and park next to it (38.463849,-77.752091). The wide trail to the pond is to the left of the kiosk.

Canoe/Kayak Comment: It is not that far down the hill to get to the lake. If you do not want to fish it from the shore, it would not take that much energy to drop a canoe or kayak in the water.

Environment and Fish

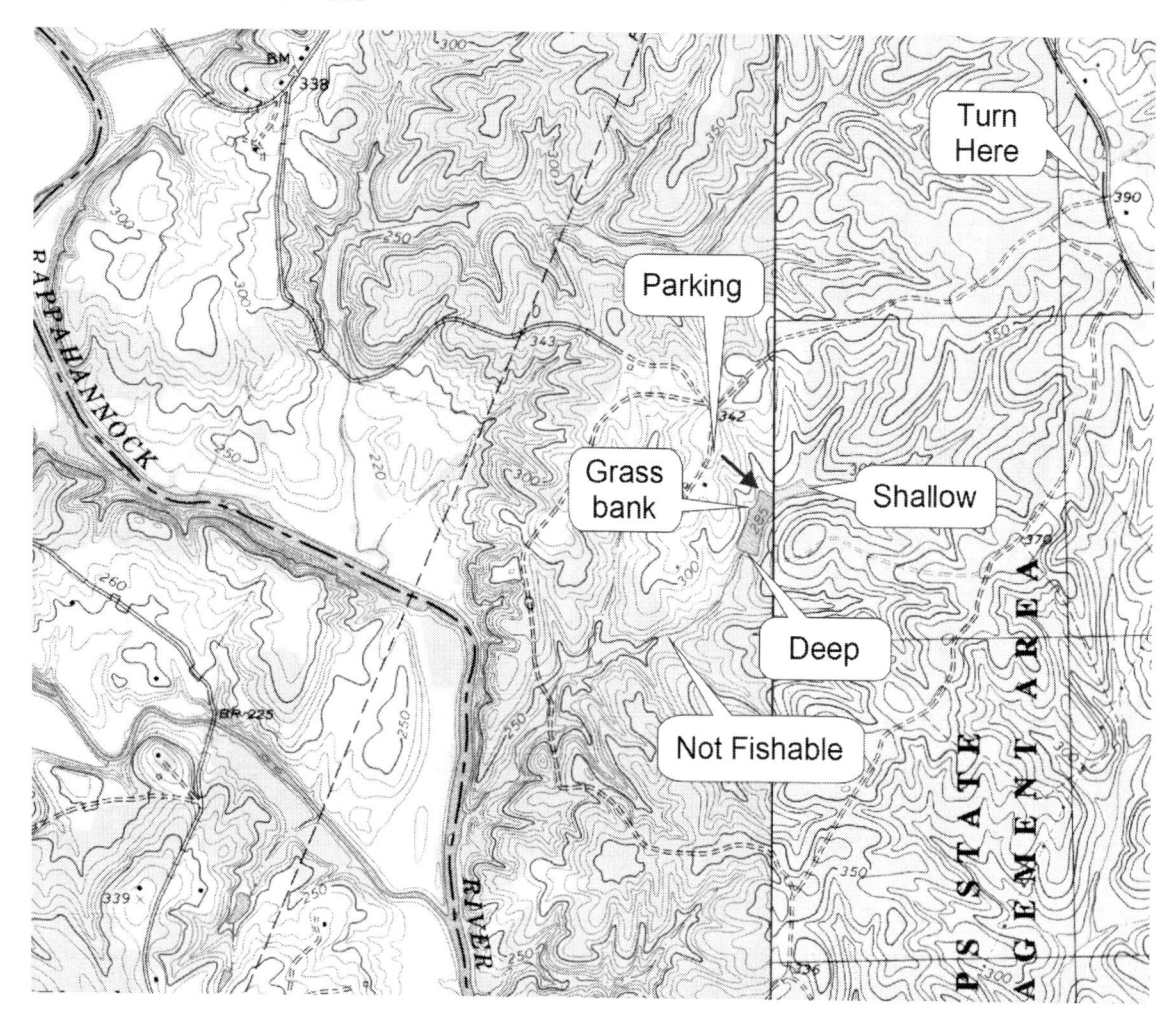

The Phelps WMA bass pond is a nice diversion from fishing the Rappahannock. In fact, if you come to Phelps with the intention of fishing the Rappahannock in the afternoon or evening, the pond is a great place to warm up and enjoy a picnic lunch on the manicured slopes that lead to the lake. Upfront, there is not much to this lake. It is a small three-acre impoundment that was created so far in the past that no one really knows its birthday. The pond is on the center section of the wildlife management area that includes the old plantation buildings constructed in the Civil War era.

The intent of the VDGIF is to develop the pond into a trophy panfish fishery and plans include the installation of a solar fish feeder to encourage development. In addition to bluegill, the lake holds largemouth bass, redear sunfish and channel catfish whose population is augmented by an annual stocking. Sadly, the catfish have limited natural reproduction in the lake. This is not a problem with the other species of fish.

The VDGIF permits anglers to fish from boats on the pond, but they must be carried to the water's edge. There is no boat ramp, but that is not a problem since the only boats appropriate are canoes and kayaks.

A short walk down the grassy road puts you at the base of the "L" that defines the overall architecture of the lake (38.462329,-77.750418). The western bank is uniformly accessible and bordered by grass fields that run up a gently sloping hill. Both fly and spin anglers will have no problem casting from the shore. However, as soon as you move to the eastern shore, the bank narrows with dense forests eliminating all possibility of a normal fly rod backcast. If you are a fly rodder, you need to be good at executing a roll cast to fish from the eastern shore. Spin anglers will have no problem anywhere on the lake.

The northern end is the shallowest and the least productive. The dam and the deep water are both at the southern end of the lake (38.460741,-77.750943) and this is where the largest fish hold. The output stream that begins its journey to the main stem of the Rappahannock from the base of the dam is not fishable.

It is easy walking to reach the shoreline.

The view into the northern section of the lake shows the gentle bank that makes this the perfect family fishing location.

Likewise, the view to the south shows the dense forest on the eastern edge that limits your ability to fish the pond using fly fishing gear.

The view back towards the access point from the dam line provides a broad perspective.

Bottom Line

The Phelps WMA bass pond is a diversion, not a destination.

Kellys Ford

Google Map Coordinates: 38.477442,-77.780505

Summary Rating

Parking	**Green**	Spin Fishing	**Green**
Canoe/Kayak Launch	**Green**	Fly Fishing	**Green**
Distance to River	**Green**	Smallmouth Structure	**Green**
Can Bike to River	**Red**	Wading Distance	**Yellow**
Physical Fitness	**Yellow**	Pressure	**Red**
Scenery	**Green**	Overall	**Green**

If there is one place on the Rappahannock that everyone knows about, it is Kellys Ford. This is one of the most popular canoe/kayak launch points on the entire river and the fishing pressure mirrors that popularity.

Getting to the Stream

North: From I-66, take exit 43A onto US 29 South at Gainesville. Follow US 29 south for 25 miles to Remington and turn left on VA 651 (Freemans Ford Road). After driving through town, turn right onto VA 651 (Sumerduck Road). Follow Sumerduck for 4.5 miles to VA 620 (Edwards Shop Road). Turn right and follow the road to the river. Park on either (38.477442,-77.780505)

South: Follow US 29 north from Culpeper to turn right onto Kellys Ford Road (VA 674) prior to crossing the Rappahannock at Remington. Follow Kellys Ford Road for five miles and turn left on VA 620 (Edwards Shop Road). Park on either side of the river (38.477442,-77.780505).

While there is parking on both sides of the river, the best one to use for wading is the lot on the east side. The water is deep next to the other lot.

Canoe/Kayak Comment: There is an improved boat launch that includes wooden stairs and a canoe slide on the southwest side of the bridge.

Environment and Fish

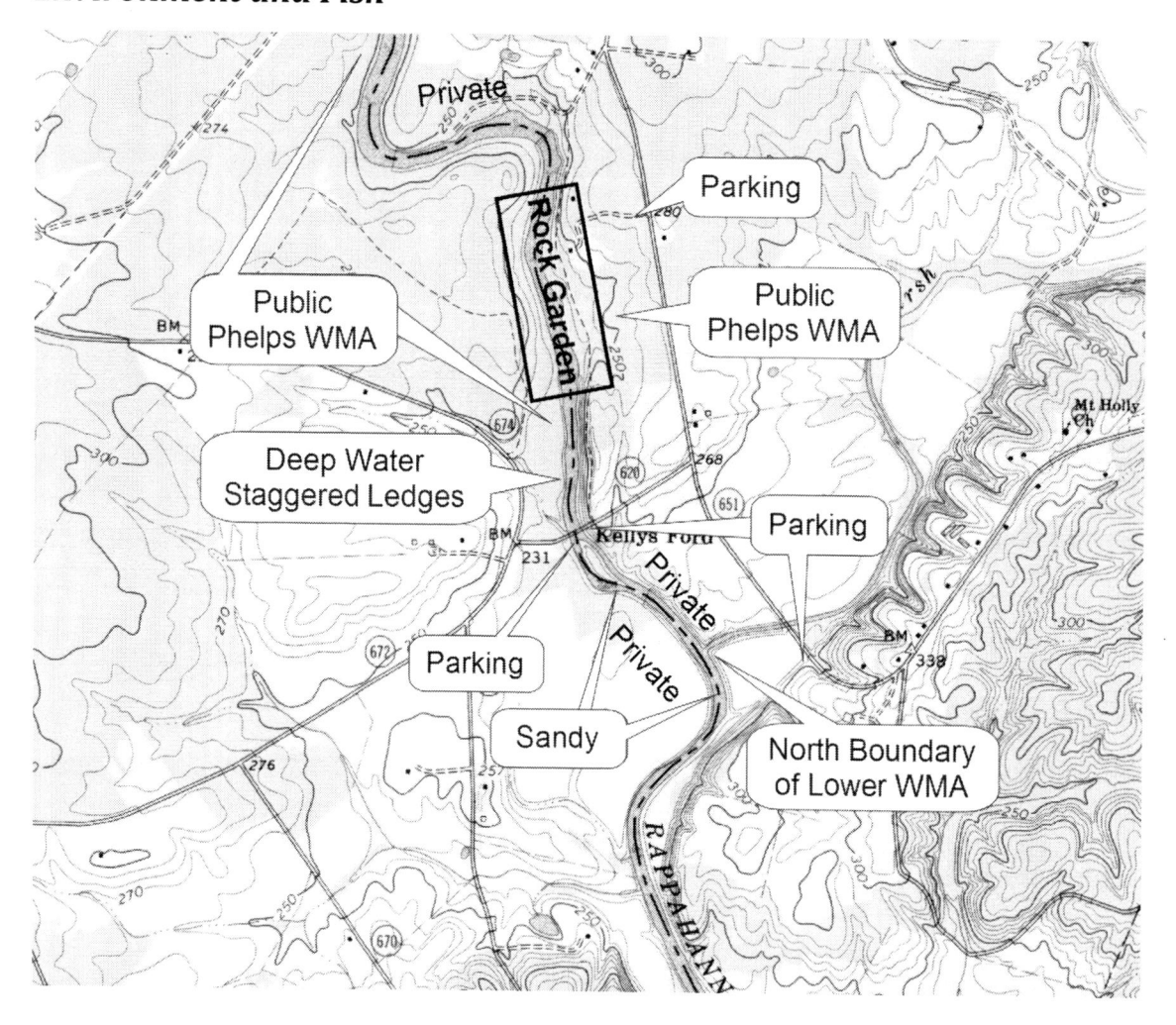

I continue to be amazed at the dramatic difference in fishing quality the Rappahannock offers based on the simple choice of moving up or downriver. Upstream is the clear winner at Kellys Ford. It features everything you would want in terms of rocky smallmouth structure and is a stark contrast to the flat, uninteresting water within wading distance downstream.

Upstream

Leave the parking lot at the western end to climb onto a narrow, but well-defined, trail that leads to the river. There is nothing to prevent you from beginning right away since the entire section experiences heavy pressure. Your first opportunity to fish is immediately underneath the bridge where there is a sand island that separates the shore from the main stem of the river. Fish the channel and begin to wade upstream along the right bank. At normal water levels, you will be closed out fairly quickly, but when the water is low, use the sandbar that extends one hundred feet up the eastern bank to thoroughly cover the deep water that parallels the western shore.

If you decide to walk upriver to move away from the parking area, continue to follow the trail until it reaches the first main set of rapids at 38.478698,-77.780741. This is the first of two primary fish collection points on the river prior to moving into the "rock garden" farther upstream. You can walk out on the shelf created by the terrain feature and pepper the deep hole immediately downstream. It is uniformly deep across the entire river. 20 feet upstream, there is another small set of rapids and the area between the two ridgelines has plenty of rocks and deep holes. Unless you use the ledges, you will be unable to wade.

Hop back on the trail and follow it to the second major set of rapids at 38.479921,-77.780547. Climb hand over foot onto the large boulders that form the eastern base of the ledge to move out and hit the main stem of the river. Immediately downstream of the largest is a deep, still pool that is usually very productive. Other than that, move as far onto the ledge as safety allows and fish both up and downstream.

At this point, the trail along the eastern shoreline essentially disappears into thick brush that is overgrown with poison ivy. Dodging that evil weed as best you can, continue to push through to eventually pick up a faint game trail that allows easy passage along the river for the next 50 yards. It disappears again and you must revert to bushwhacking until the trail finally reemerges at 38.48371,-77.78110.

A point of interest unrelated to fishing occurs at 38.48508,-77.78169 where you encounter something totally unexpected. The trail lurches to the right away from the river and enters a dense, tall stand of bamboo. It is thick. Twenty feet into it you might conclude you are in a jungle instead of fishing for smallmouth along the Rappahannock River. The bamboo should be the upper boundary of your hike since the river upstream is much closer to the Hogue Tract discussed in the next chapter

Regardless of the ease of walking, the river offers spectacular structure and good fishing that seems to hold up despite the pressure and the popularity. Fish anywhere that looks good because it will be.

The view from the first major ledge hints of the promise upstream at 342 cfs.

It is mostly flat water back to the bridge. Note the thick vegetation on the shore that limits mobility. Fish the deep water below the major break.

Upstream of the second major ledge, the river begins to adopt the ideal smallmouth structure you expect in the Rappahannock.

Opposite the bamboo forest, the river widens into a deep lake. Use the rocks and ledges to move out into the center.

This thin, grassy ledge is your highway to superb fishing in the middle.

The rocks continue farther upstream into the Hogue Tract.

It is amazing to see the bamboo forest that grows next to the river at the upper end.

It is dense, thick and worth a visit just to see what one looks like.

Downstream

If you fish the upstream section before you venture down, prepare to be disappointed. Like the parking lot on the east side of the river, the lot associated with the canoe launch is easily accessible and supports a significant number of vehicles, primarily catering to the floating crowd.

The first place to fish is along the shoreline up to the bridge. It is normally deep on the western bank and you may not find a good place to wade into the water directly from the parking area. In fact, many people park at the other lot and wade downstream, leveraging the shallow ledge that extends into the middle of the river and onto a major sandbar directly in front of the launch. You can fish the deep channel that holds to the western bank from that sandbar. A point of caution is that all the property to the south of the road, with the small exception of the parking lot itself, is private property. The wildlife management area does not start again until 38.474142,-77.775267, approximately 1,500 feet downstream and, even then, is only on the eastern bank. Therefore, if you intend to begin wading from the canoe launch, you must ignore the well beaten trail that extends down the western shoreline that is fully and completely populated with "posted" signs and enter the river to walk down the muddy shoreline. Depending on the water levels, that can be problematic since it involves a difficult slog through knee-deep muck.

All these words basically communicate that if you want to fish downstream, park at the lot on the other side of the river and walk under the bridge and onto the sandbar. At normal water levels, the sandbar extends from 38.477179,-77.780232 600 feet downriver to 38.475999,-77.778741. Ignore the small side channel that runs along the west bank and devote your full attention to the east. The river bottom is a mix of sand and rocks with the sand increasing the farther you go downstream. If you decide to persist, fish the channels and the shore where the water deepens underneath the overhanging vegetation. Eventually, the river takes a bend to the south and forms a deep lake that prohibits further downward movement.

If you really want to fish from this point downstream, you should park in the Phelps WMA parking area on the southwest side of Marsh Run off Sumerduck road at 38.474427,-77.772783. Follow the road from the parking lot 700 feet to the south and it eventually leads to the bend where there is a small rocky island just downstream.

The view looking up to the bridge shows the major island in the middle near the launch.

Downstream, the river runs over a mix of sand and cobble.

The perspective does not change into the bend at 342 cfs.

Farther into the bend...

Bottom Line

Despite the pressure, Kellys Ford continues to hold up as a pretty good fishing location. Upstream is clearly the winner and you should fish in that direction.

Hogue Tract

Google Map Coordinates: 38.48697,-77.78154

Summary Rating

Parking	Green	Spin Fishing	Green
Canoe/Kayak Launch	Red	Fly Fishing	Green
Distance to River	Yellow	Smallmouth Structure	Green
Can Bike to River	Green	Wading Distance	Green
Physical Fitness	Red	Pressure	Yellow
Scenery	Green	Overall	Green

The Hogue Tract is the last superb fishing the Rappahannock will offer up.

Getting to the Stream

North: From I-66, take exit 43A onto US 29 South at Gainesville. Follow US 29 south for 25 miles to Remington amd turn left on VA 651 (Freemans Ford Road). After driving through town, turn right onto VA 651 (Sumerduck Road). Follow Sumerduck for 3.7 miles to the parking area on the right (38.486483,-77.778032).

South: Follow US 29 north from Culpeper to turn right onto Kellys Ford Road (VA 674) prior to crossing the Rappahannock at Remington. Follow Kellys Ford Road for five miles and turn left on VA 620 (Edwards Shop Road). Once across the river, turn left on Sumerduck Road and head north. The parking area is on the left approximately 0.8 miles from the turn (38.486483,-77.778032).

From the parking lot, walk west and ignore the two major side trails that extend off to the north. Your target is the end of the improved road at 38.486556,-77.779953. From there, pick up the small trail leading down to the river.

Canoe/Kayak Comment: The long hike down to the river's edge eliminates this as a potential put-in or take-out.

Environment and Fish

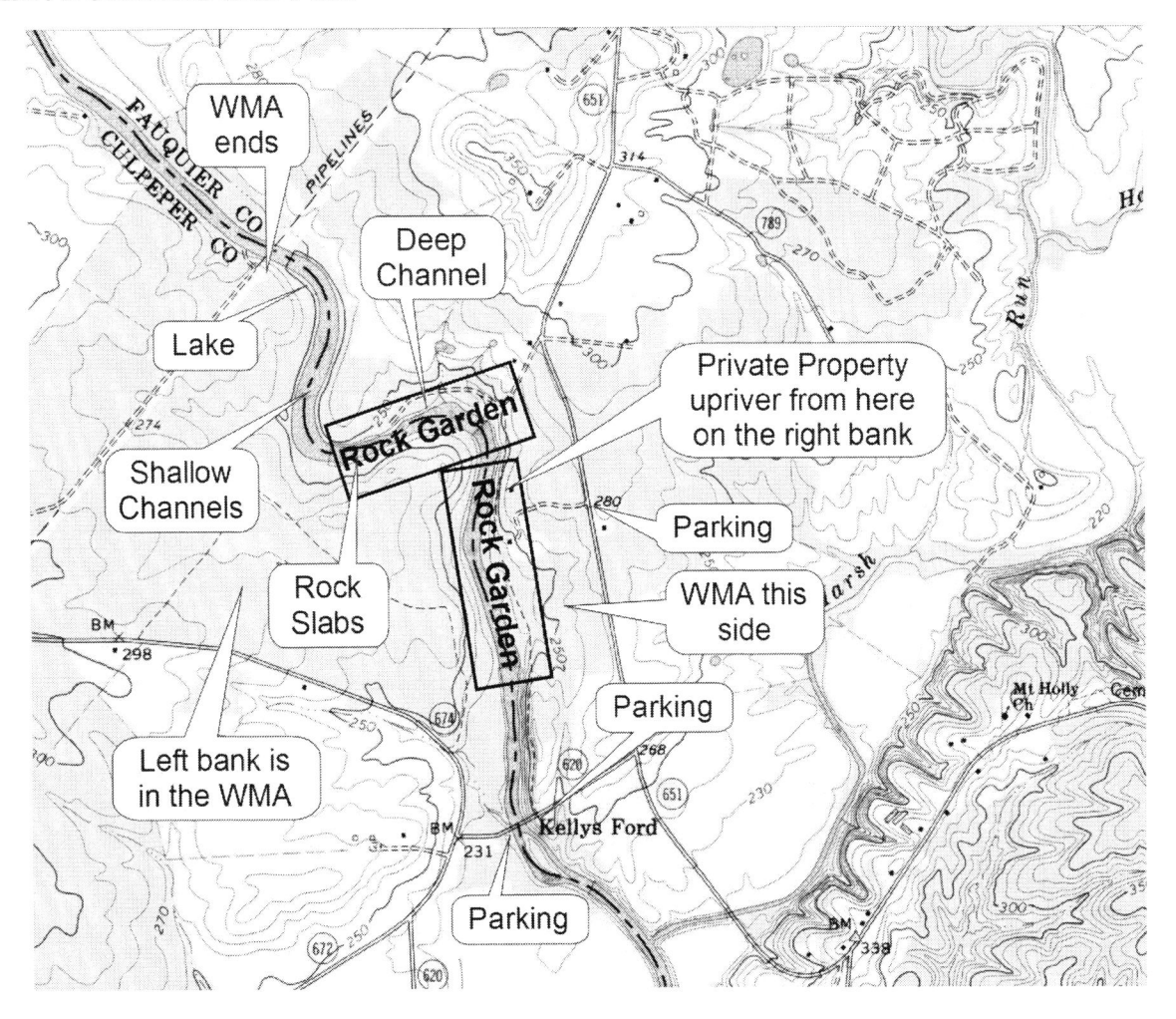

[Map showing area around Kellys Ford with labels: WMA ends, Deep Channel, Lake, Rock Garden, Shallow Channels, Rock Slabs, Rock Garden, Private Property upriver from here on the right bank, Parking, WMA this side, Parking, Left bank is in the WMA, Kellys Ford, Parking]

This entire section, both up and downriver from where the trail ends on the bank, is superb smallmouth water. You can wander for hours fishing all of the varied structure within a two mile radius. Upstream or down? Both are great choices.

Upstream

It does not really matter where you burst out from the woods onto the water, anywhere is a good place to start. Likewise, there is no need to walk any additional distance to put pressure behind. While this location is popular, the structure is varied and the fish population robust - you do not have to worry about that issue.

The fact that the upstream section is densely packed with ledges and rocks makes it hard to provide advice since all the key landmarks merge together into a conglomeration of boulders that frame narrower runs leading to prolific pools. But, there are a few landmarks that provide some rough orientation. If you follow the main trail, the first major set of ledges occurs at 38.487584,-77.781546. These provide the middle boundary that breaks the deep water at the trailhead in half. You may find it difficult to wade across the river at this point, but that should not prevent you from fishing out into the center of the channel as far as you can. Continue up the right bank and the lake above this first landmark eventually evaporates into a muddled mix of boulders where the river begins to transition around the corner to the west. At normal water levels, this is the first opportunity to cross the river. Take advantage of a crossing as soon as it presents itself and use the western shore as your base of operations. As the river turns the corner, private property starts on the eastern bank. The entire western bank remains within the wildlife management area.

After fishing through the corner and experiencing the joy of exposing its convoluted secrets, there is a transition point at 38.48898,-77.78322 where the river runs directly west. There are fewer shallow stretches and more deep channels that present a challenge to negotiate. I prefer to wade along the southern shoreline to move upstream and launch attacks perpendicular to the north to hit the better spots. It is problematic to give advice on this section because of the variation in depth associated with different water levels. However, when in doubt, stay south. The water along the northern shoreline is usually deep and difficult to wade through. If you go that way, you will be forced to trespass on the private property that lines the northern bank.

At 38.488556,-77.784791, there is a 50 foot wide jumble of large boulders that define the best spot. Immediately downstream is deep water with major channels. Walk onto the rocks to throw as far into them as possible. Looking upstream, the river compresses and shrinks from being 100 feet or wider downstream to 70 feet as it runs through a narrow passage where the shorelines pinches together. The spot, 38.488252,-77.785945, is easy to identify by the massive slabs of rock that litter the center of the river. It is problematic to fish the fast water that surrounds them and you may find yourself having to stay close to the bank to get by. Continue to fish upriver to the bend (38.488006,-77.787396) where sand and boulders create a buffer that bounces the river north and starts the compression that extends downriver for the next 300 feet. At that point, your fishing experience changes.

Whereas, up to now, the river has been more deep than shallow, upstream for the next 1,100 feet the opposite is true. Instead of being deep, the runs are shallower. The good news is that it continues to hold bass and sunfish. Beyond the bend, there is no distinctive landmark until you stumble up to the northern limit of wading created by the lake at 38.491297,-77.787593. At the lake, your frustration will grow because, on a clear water day, you can see scattered boulders beneath the deep surface that must hold the largest fish in this section. The best you can do is to stay against the left bank and fish upstream approximately 25 yards, throwing into the deep water of the center channel.

It is easy to be spoiled with views like this after you break out of the brush. This is the upstream perspective.

The downstream vista is equally compelling at 282 cfs.

Grass islands and rocks define an infinite number of channels. It is deep on the right-hand bank, so move left as soon as you can.

The rock slabs emerge at the center of this picture. The lake in the foreground is extremely productive.

The run up to the lake is shallow and chiseled by the innumerable rocks. You can pick up fish if you find the deep spots.

At the lake, it is too deep to move any farther. Move to the left and fish as far into the lake as you can wade (282 cfs).

Downstream

The downstream experience is merely an extension of the description upstream from Kellys Ford. After fishing the lake at the trailhead, the only landmark before reaching the stand of bamboo mentioned in the prior chapter is the start of the dense rock garden at 38.486749,-77.781831. The rock garden provides an unlimited number of variations of rock–channel–pool combinations. Move downstream. If the water levels cooperate, leverage the eastern shoreline to slide back and forth across the breadth of the river. You may encounter swimmers who enjoy floating the short distance from the Hogue Tract down to the Kellys Ford bridge. If you do, turn your rod and fish upstream.

Below the initial rock garden and above the stand of bamboo, the river creates a 400 foot long lake that is speckled with random boulders, creating associated channels and good spots. There are no landmarks to orient on – just target the boulders and fish the pools and channels.

Bottom Line

Use the Hogue Tract to make a short walk into the densest rock structure on the upper river. This is a good spot to fish.

Remington

Google Map Coordinates: 38.530068,-77.813646

Summary Rating

Parking	Yellow	Spin Fishing	Green
Canoe/Kayak Launch	Yellow	Fly Fishing	Green
Distance to River	Yellow	Smallmouth Structure	Yellow
Can Bike to River	Green	Wading Distance	Green
Physical Fitness	Red	Pressure	Red
Scenery	Red	Overall	Yellow

Upstream is good and represents one of the last places with a good burst of rocks that actually hold fish. Downstream beyond the railroad bridge is a waste of time. Expect to see swimmers during the summer.

Getting to the Stream

North: From I-66, take exit 43A onto US 29 South at Gainesville. Follow US 29 south for 25 miles to Remington. Go across the river and make an immediate left onto Business 29.

South: Follow US 29 north from Culpeper to turn right onto Business 29 immediately prior to crossing the river.

Warning! Do not park adjacent to the river on Business 29. The landowner on the southwest side of the river has convinced the Department of Transportation to post "no parking" signs every few feet and is reputed to be aggressive in his enforcement. Instead, continue into the town of Remington and park in the empty lot across the street from the Andes Market & Deli. If you ask inside, they will also let you park by the back fence if you prefer to be off the main road. Obviously, we want to encourage this flexibility and I urge you to buy a sandwich or something else at the deli. Once parked, walk the thousand feet back to the river.

In the near future, the Rappahannock Station Battlefield Park will open. It will commemorate two battles that were fought in Remington for control of the bridge. Of note to anglers is that the Park will provide the only public access to the Rappahannock River in Fauquier County. Once it is open, you will not have to slide down the steep bank using the VDOT easement to reach the river. There should be formal parking as well as an improved canoe/kayak launch in the vicinity of US 29.

Canoe/Kayak Comment: If you are quick, you can pull off on the side of the road near the bridge and drop your boat. Drive farther into Remington, park and return. Drag it down the steep hill to launch under the bridge. I would avoid doing this on the south side of the bridge as a result of the enthusiastic enforcement of the no parking regulation in that area.

Environment and Fish

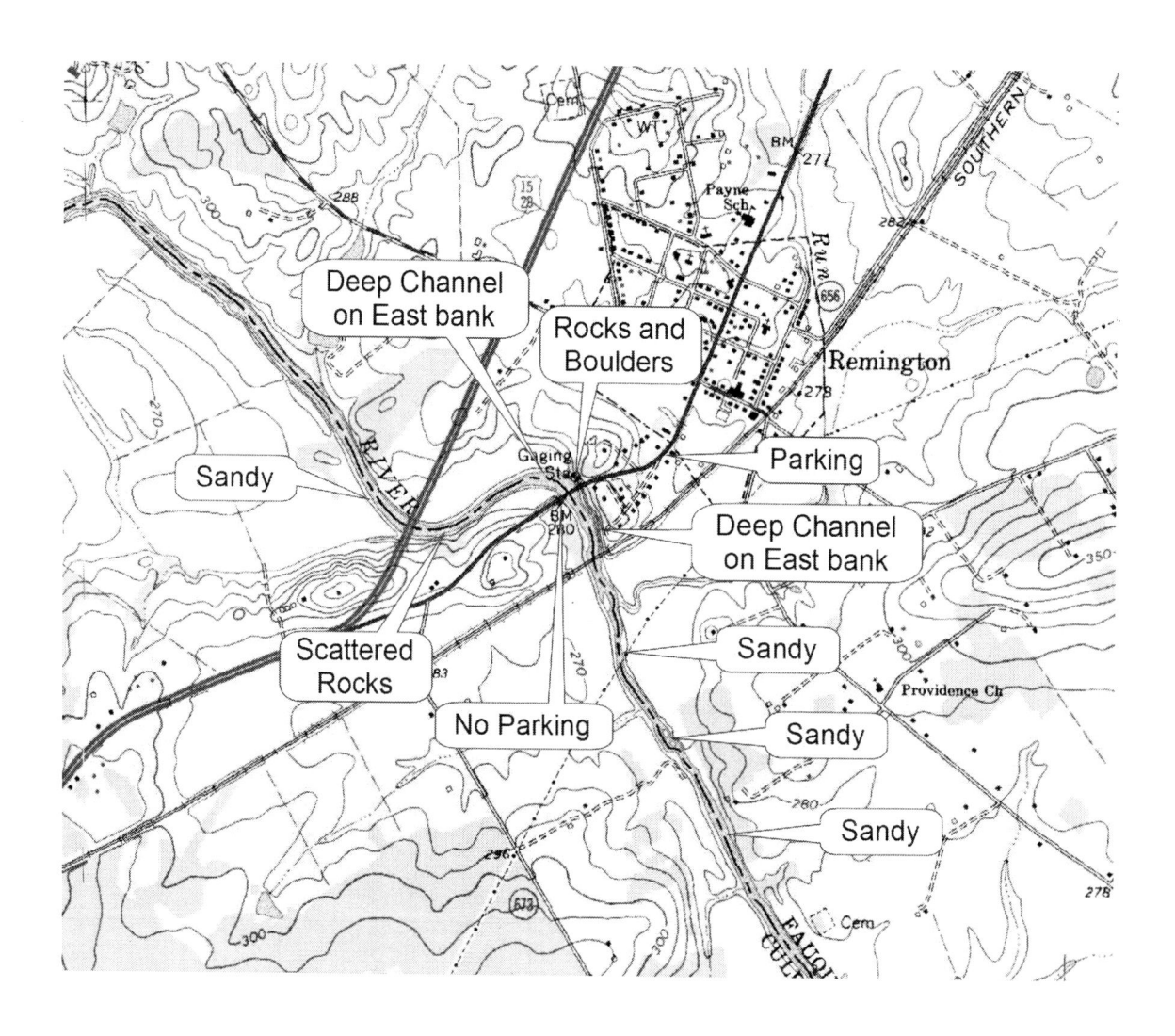

Upstream

You will get the wrong impression of Remington if you base your opinion on what you see from the bridge as you zip over it. The only thing visible is the sandy bottom that decorates the left bank. What is not obvious is that the area immediately below the bridge, paralleling the right bank up to a tangle of fallen logs, is perfect smallmouth habitat. To fish upstream, enter from the eastern side and begin casting as soon as you enter the water. Depending on the time of day, you may have to dodge around families of swimmers. They usually stick to the sandbar on the west side and avoid the rocky area on the right bank. So ignore them and throw to the bank.

Since the water is deep along the eastern bank, you have to find a shallow line to walk at a 45° angle into the center of the river. Your goal is to find a perch that will allow you to walk up the center while casting to the right. At 38.53050,-77.81464, there is a dramatic change in the bottom where it makes an instant switch from being remarkably deep to exceedingly shallow. Use it as the boundary that defines the orbit pattern. Slide along the line of maximum depth based on your ability to wade and circle the right bank. Even though you are within sight of the swimmers, you can easily spend an hour catching decent fish.

After passing the second logjam (38.530576,-77.815449), move to the right since the deep channel switches to the left. Fish each logjam as you walk towards the rocks in the distance. However, I recommend that you not spend a lot of time on them as a result of the continued sandy bottom that discourages smallmouth. At 38.53034,-77.81589, move to the extreme right bank to make continued progress upriver. As you encounter deep water and move to the right, the bottom changes from being sand to a mix of boulders interspersed with sand and small rocks huddling under water running three feet deep. Concentrate on the center and the left. Carry on upriver, peppering the rock structure all the way to the large tree that hangs precariously over the center of the river. Near the tree, there are some noticeable rocks that peek above the surface.

Starting where the rocks begin, the river becomes shallow and is lucky to achieve a depth of two feet in most places. However that should not discourage you. The bottom is pockmarked with small holes covered with vegetation and each has the potential to hold good fish.

It is not until you start to approach the bend and the US 29 bridge that the river transitions into a shelf at 38.52938,-77.81762. There are smallmouth throughout this section. Near the flat rock shelf, move to the right and fish to the left. There are a number of deep cuts that run up to three feet deep across the pockmarked section on the left. Nearer the bridge, the bottom returns to sand. Although it continues to be worth fishing the left side, you will not find any smallmouth on the right.

Once above the flat rock shelf, the deep section is on the left. While the right bank remains sandy, the left bank is a mix of flat rock with cuts demonstrating depths that range up to four feet. Fish that side as you walk up to the bridge. The closer you get to the bridge, the deeper the water gets, forcing you to the right bank. To make matters worse, the bottom switches back to sand with only random rocks visible at the bridge. Uncharacteristically, there are no deep holes or pools to exploit under the bridge. You are now a little over 0.5 miles from the entry point. Looking upstream, the river is almost 100% sand with the deep channel continuing on the left. In the summer, the sandbars on the right stretch upstream to disappear in the distance. If you decide to go farther than the US 29 bridge, fish the three log tangles just upriver. However, I do not recommend going any farther given the nature of the bottom and the quality of the fishing.

The area under the bridge is a popular place for swimmers at 34 cfs.

Begin fishing immediately upstream into the rocks that line the right bank.

Continue to fish the right bank all the way through the logjam at the right of the picture.

Beyond the jam, look for the deep channel and the structure (72 cfs).

There is good water near the US 29 bridge where some rocks litter the bottom.

Upstream of the bridge is a waste of time.

Downstream

If you make the mistake of entering the river from the Remington side of the bridge, you will not be able to get very far downstream. The river is deep with clustered, large boulders strewn throughout the eastern bank all the way down to the overhanging tree - recognizable by the rope swing suspended from its upper reaches. The immediate structure is phenomenal. There are large, flat rocks just under the surface separated by yawning chasms that conspire to defeat an attack launched parallel to the shoreline. If you enter the river from the east, move directly away from the shore towards the middle bridge pylon and fish downstream. Loop around to the extent the depth permits to fish consistently against the east bank.

There is a grass bed that has a steep drop-off leading towards the middle of the river. In high water, this is where you may be closed out. However, if you can wiggle around, fish the bank underneath the overhanging tree and the subsequent structure all the way down to an old bridge piling on the west bank approximately one hundred feet from the main bridge. The rocks continue on the east.

There is a deep spot next to a prominent cluster of rocks on the left bank across from the old bridge piling. Even though it is very deep, it is only worth a cast or two based on the large number of trails that converge on it, indicating intense pressure. Downstream, the rocks return and the river deepens in the middle. It is worth fishing the center down to the gradient break underneath the railroad bridge. Approaching the top of the gradient break, keep your focus on the left bank. The right bank continues to be a shallow, sandy shelf without any interesting rock structure. The left bank features scattered boulders and a gradually increasing amount of smaller subsurface rocks close to the railroad bridge. The beaten trails continue all the way down to the railroad bridge confirming that the Remington side of the river is heavily fished. That said, throw a cast or two at the grass bed where it pokes out just upstream of the railroad bridge.

At the base of the gradient break near the bridge, a broad lake stretches into the downstream distance. There is a deep cut on the right that runs next to the grass bed, feeding a hole underneath the bridge piling and an even deeper hole to the left. Once you fish 180°, move to the left to walk out on the sandbar that divides the river into two channels. Be sure to fish ahead of yourself against the grass on the left. While it is only a foot or two deep, the cover provided by the underwater vegetation is compelling and attracts fish. As you walk down the sandbar, ignore the left channel and focus on the right.

A set of power lines crosses the river in the distance at 38.524962,-77.811595. Usually, that would generate some interest because, for some reason, fishing underneath power lines is usually pretty good. With every step you take towards the power line, you begin to suspect that your excitement was premature. At a gage reading of 34 cfs, the river is terminally shallow and can be measured in inches instead of feet. While there is a small deep area on the right bank underneath the power line, if the summer has been hot, do not expect to find any smallmouth there.

After you fish the small hole underneath the power line, cast your gaze downriver to the cluster of rocks and rough water that indicates riffles approximately a quarter mile downstream (38.522511,-77.809479). Typically, that would signal smallmouth habitat with deep water at the base of the riffle. Save your energy and do not walk any farther. Those riffles mark the one mile point from your vehicle and for the last half mile, you have been sloshing through shallow water with your feet sinking into soft sand. There is nothing interesting farther downstream. In fact, it is not worth going any farther than the railroad bridge.

In terms of full disclosure, other people have told me they have been successful farther downstream. Therefore, you may want to risk the additional hike to reach the area near 38.510945,-77.800639 where Strodes Mill Road points to the river from the east and rocks and vegetation return briefly. They did say they caught some big ones there....

The area immediately downstream of the bridge is the deepest. Work it from the opposite bank instead of teetering on the rocks.

View down to the railroad bridge gives the correct impression of depth at 34 cfs.

Under the bridge, the sandbars emerge downstream. Fish the deep hole to the left.

Do not ignore the tail end of the gradient break under the bridge.

The downstream sandbars on the right indicate poor fishing.

This may look deep, but it is tragically shallow and totally sandy.

There is one solitary good spot underneath the power line.

Below the power line, it is shallow to the point of being a waste of time.

Bottom Line

If you can get here early before the swimmers show up, the fishing upstream from the bridge is good. While there are fish downstream next to the eastern bank, that small spot experiences significant pressure as a result of the trail that runs along a high ridgeline above the water. There is no equivalent trail on the upstream side.

Lakota (Freeman Ford)

Google Map Coordinates: 38.582979,-77.875471

Summary Rating

Parking	**Red**	Spin Fishing	**Green**
Canoe/Kayak Launch	**Green**	Fly Fishing	**Green**
Distance to River	**Green**	Smallmouth Structure	**Red**
Can Bike to River	**Red**	Wading Distance	**Green**
Physical Fitness	**Green**	Pressure	**Yellow**
Scenery	**Yellow**	Overall	**Red**

Freemans Ford is not worth getting out of the car to fish. There is nothing good to say about this particular location.

Getting to the Stream

From US 15/US 29 turn north onto VA 651 (Freemans Ford Road) near Remington. Follow VA 651 north for approximately five miles to the bridge crossing at 38.582979,-77.875471. Park on the wide shoulder approximately 60 feet east of the river.

Canoe/Kayak Comment: The parking on the side of the road is close enough to the water to make this a candidate location to launch a boat. It is totally unimproved and will require a portage of approximately 100 feet to get to the water's edge.

Environment and Fish

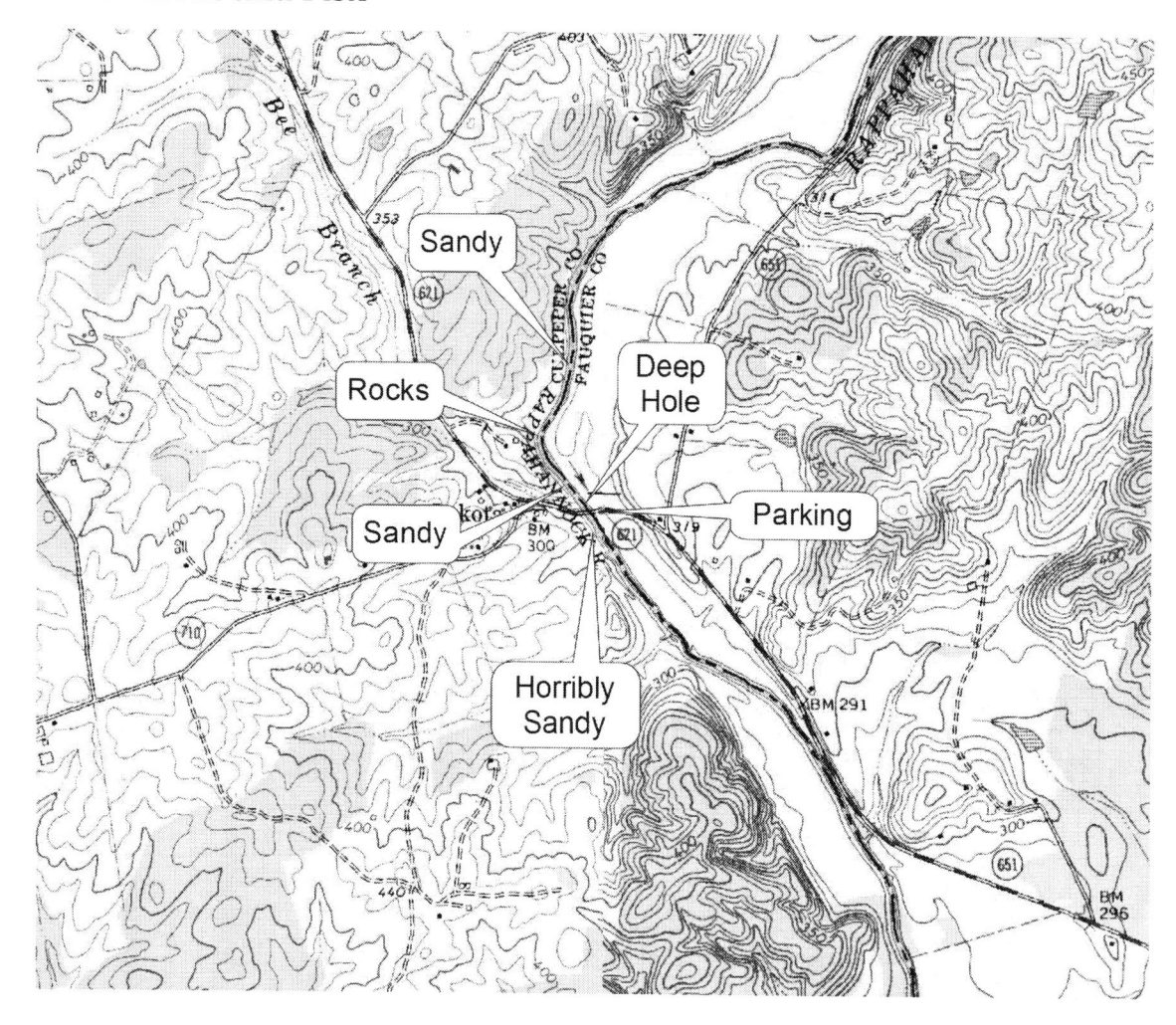

Upstream

To fish upstream, start off on the west side of the bridge where there is a rocky run that is approximately a foot deep. Fish up around the edge of the logjam that wraps around the middle piling. There is a small lake that backs up above the bridge with deep water on the left. You can still wade through it by starting from the right and easing to the center. There is plenty of overhanging vegetation on the right bank that provides perfect holding areas for fish during the heat of the afternoon. Given the sandy bottom, you will not encounter many smallmouth, but you will catch as many sunfish and fallfish as you care to pull in. The further upstream you go, the deeper it gets, eventually being waist deep at the bend in the river. If the water is high, you may have to edge close to the bank to get beyond that particular spot.

The corner defines the best water at Freeman Ford (38.585186,-77.877352). In fact, it is the first place where you have a remote chance of picking up a smallmouth. Where the water is deeper than a foot, it will be infested with sunfish and fallfish. Around the bend, the water level drops to less than a foot and the bottom continues to be a sandy into the distance. There is a brief interlude of rocks upstream of the bend. Given the persistent sand upstream, it is not worth the energy to go any farther than this and, actually, it wasn't worth it to come even this far.

There is a good hole just upstream on the bridge on the west bank. Fish the logjam carefully and move into the deep area upstream (382 cfs).

The bottom is 100% sand and the only opportunity to catch fish is near the fallen logs on either shore (72 cfs).

At the bend, this fallen log holds the largest fish.

Beyond the log, the river is mostly sand with a few scattered rocks.

Downstream

While there is a nice one to two foot deep pool immediately underneath the bridge, as soon as you walk 100 yards downstream, the Rappahannock loses its energy and volume and fails to create any pools or runs large enough to hold anything interesting to catch. It is nothing but sand, shallow channels and the standard collection of sunfish and fallfish. Absolutely boring, totally uninteresting and certainly not worth the gas or the energy to get here.

Fish in the pool to the left as well as the run on the right underneath the tree (72 cfs).

This is the same location at the more interesting water level of 382 cfs.

The river narrows and runs slow over the sandy bottom.

But, even that peters out when the river becomes ankle-deep.

Bottom Line

An absolute waste of time. Words cannot describe how bad this particular location is.

Springs Road (VA 802)

Google Map Coordinates: 38.648542,-77.871501

Summary Rating

Parking	**Red**	Spin Fishing	**Green**
Canoe/Kayak Launch	**Green**	Fly Fishing	**Green**
Distance to River	**Green**	Smallmouth Structure	**Red**
Can Bike to River	**Red**	Wading Distance	**Green**
Physical Fitness	**Green**	Pressure	**Green**
Scenery	**Red**	Overall	**Red**

This location is not worth the cost of the gas. There are no rocks or other attractive habitat. The bottom is nothing but sand and if you fish here, all you will catch are fallfish and sunfish.

Getting to the Stream

North: From I-66 westbound, take exit 43B onto US 29 (Lee Highway) south towards Warrenton. Stay on US 29 past Warrenton to turn right on VA 687 (Opal Road). Follow Opal Road until it dead ends on Springs Road at a "T" intersection. Turn left on Springs Road and follow it to the bridge over the Rappahannock (38.648542,-77.871501).

South: From Follow US 29 (Lee Highway) north towards Warrenton. Turn left on VA 687 (Opal Road). Follow Opal Road until it dead ends on Springs Road at a "T" intersection. Turn left on Springs Road and follow it to the bridge over the Rappahannock (38.648542,-77.871501).

Immediately prior to reaching the bridge from the east, pull off in the wide spot on the right side. It will fit approximately two vehicles. From there, you have the choice of following the beaten trail that leads directly to the river across private property or skinny along the guardrail to stay within the VDOT easement (recommended). This is a well used access point with the key indicator being the park bench that somebody positioned underneath the bridge. Unless you need to take a break, ignore the bench and enter the river.

Canoe/Kayak Comment: The parking on the side of the road is close enough to the water to make this a candidate location to launch a boat. It is totally unimproved and will require a portage of approximately 100 feet to get to the water's edge.

Environment and Fish

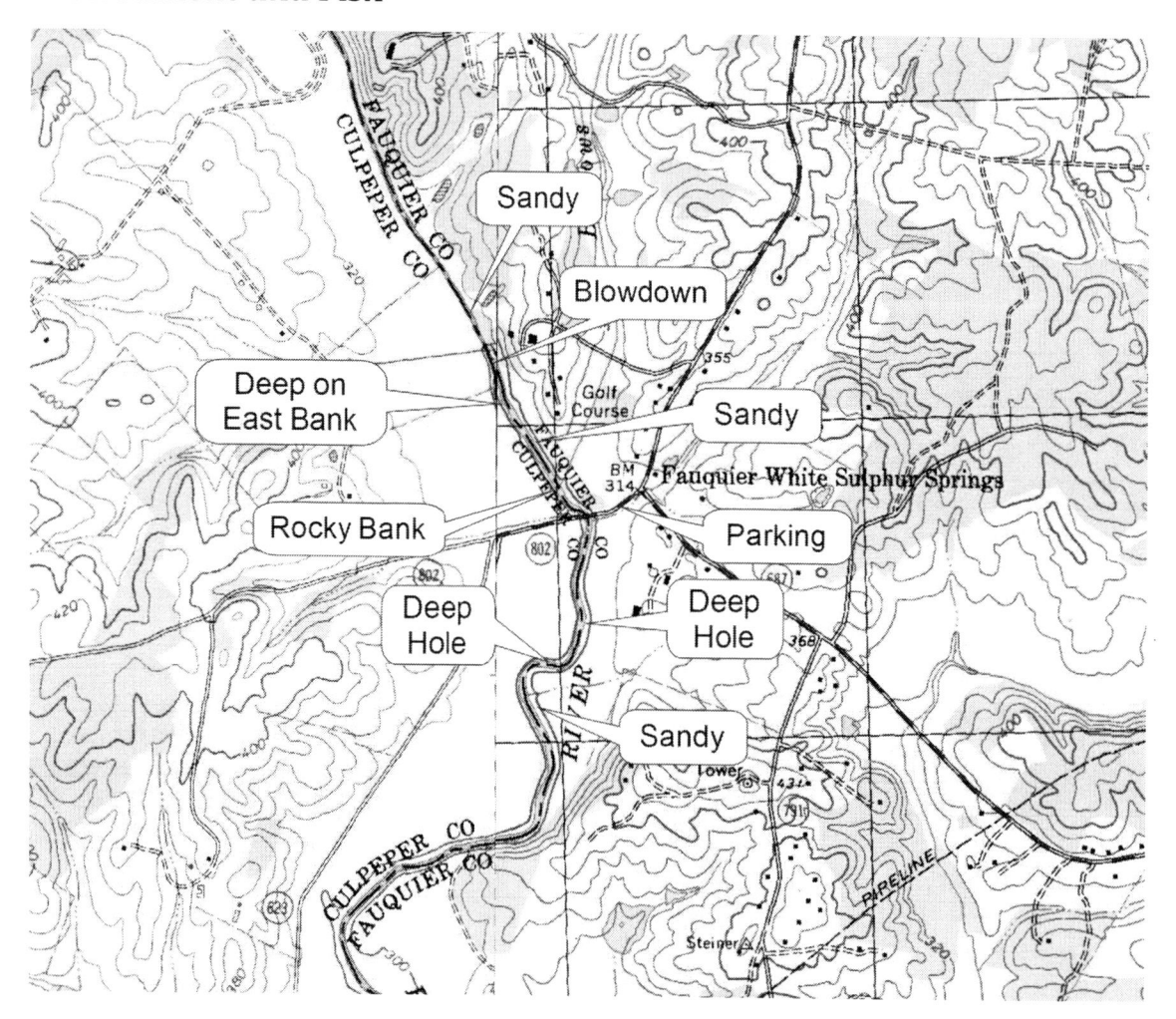

Upstream

Go directly to the left bank. Fish will hold near the low point just upstream of the bridge. The river stays consistently deep along the rocky bank stretching upstream for approximately 50 yards. Beyond that, the river makes a few turns around fallen logs and the deep water switches to the right bank.

Fish the deep run on the right side and continue upstream until you get to the large blowdown that blocks the entire river. At that spot, there are two deep holes – one on either side of the sandbar that built up in the middle of the river on the downstream side. These two spots are worth fishing, but there is nothing interesting upstream. If you go farther, notice the light beige color that confirms the bottom is consistently and interminably sandy. Without rocks, the only thing you will catch for your continued upstream effort are fallfish and sunfish.

The overhanging vegetation protecting the river offers some slim hope of good water. The rocky bank on the left begins just upstream of the bridge.

The rocky bank continues upstream.

And finally presents the only good fishing in this section (382 cfs).

Up and downstream of this log is the other good spot.

Downstream

As you swing your rod downstream, prepare for immediate disappointment. As far as you can squint into the distance, the river runs shallow across a sand bottom. There is nothing compelling to fish within walking distance. If you want to move downstream to prove this to yourself, you may as well walk a quarter mile to the head of the small riffle where a number of trees lean into the river from the right bank (38.645975,-77.871503). There is a deep pool underneath the trees that will hold any fish worth catching.

Continue downstream to the grass island that separates the river into two channels. Stay left and fish the deep spot created beyond the second grass island adjacent to a complex of fallen logs. Quickly move from that spot to the next gradient break, fishing the left bank until the water becomes terminally shallow. The river bottom is still sand and you will be lucky to catch anything, but if you keep going, the river deepens on the left bank as it makes the next turn (38.644365,-77.872469). Fish the deep hole underneath a large log and follow the flow as it transitions the depth to the right bank at the top of the next curve (38.644453,-77.873668).

At this point, you are a half mile from your vehicle and all you have seen for your effort is sand. Unless you are a glutton for punishment, turn around and head back to the bridge.

Downstream from the bridge, there appears to be enough interesting other structure to make the walk downstream worthwhile. False hope.

The deep spot is on the left of the first major grass island.

This is the last the deep spot worth fishing. The depth is on the right bank at 382 cfs.

Sand, sand, sand, sand! Not worth it.

Bottom Line

I strongly recommend you not bother to fish this location.

Warrenton - Lee Highway

Google Map Coordinates: 38.683902,-77.902422

Summary Rating

Parking	Yellow	Spin Fishing	Green
Canoe/Kayak Launch	Green	Fly Fishing	Green
Distance to River	Green	Smallmouth Structure	Yellow
Can Bike to River	Red	Wading Distance	Green
Physical Fitness	Green	Pressure	Yellow
Scenery	Green	Overall	Yellow

The fishing upstream is good for the first 50 yards. Downstream is much better.

Getting to the Stream

North: From I-66 westbound, take exit 43B onto US 29 (Lee Highway) south towards Warrenton. Take a slight right at US 15/US 29 Business south and follow it to make a right turn onto US 211 W at Frost Avenue. Follow US 211 to the bridge over the Rappahannock (38.683902,-77.902422).

South: Follow US 15/US 29 north from Charlottesville. Once beyond Culpeper, turn left on VA 666 and follow it to where it dead ends on Brandy Road. Turn left and head into Culpeper. Turn right on VA 694 (Ira Hoffman Lane). Turn right on VA 229 (Rixeyville Road) and follow it to US 211. Turn right on US 211. Follow US 211 to the bridge over the Rappahannock (38.683902,-77.902422).

On the north (Warrenton) side of the river, turn right from the westbound lane onto a small dirt road that runs down a narrow gap between the highway and a wire fence. Turn onto the road and bump into the small parking area at the base of the bridge.

Canoe/Kayak Comment: The parking is adjacent to the water. The bank is steep and requires you to slide your boat down a two to three foot drop to reach the water..

Environment and Fish

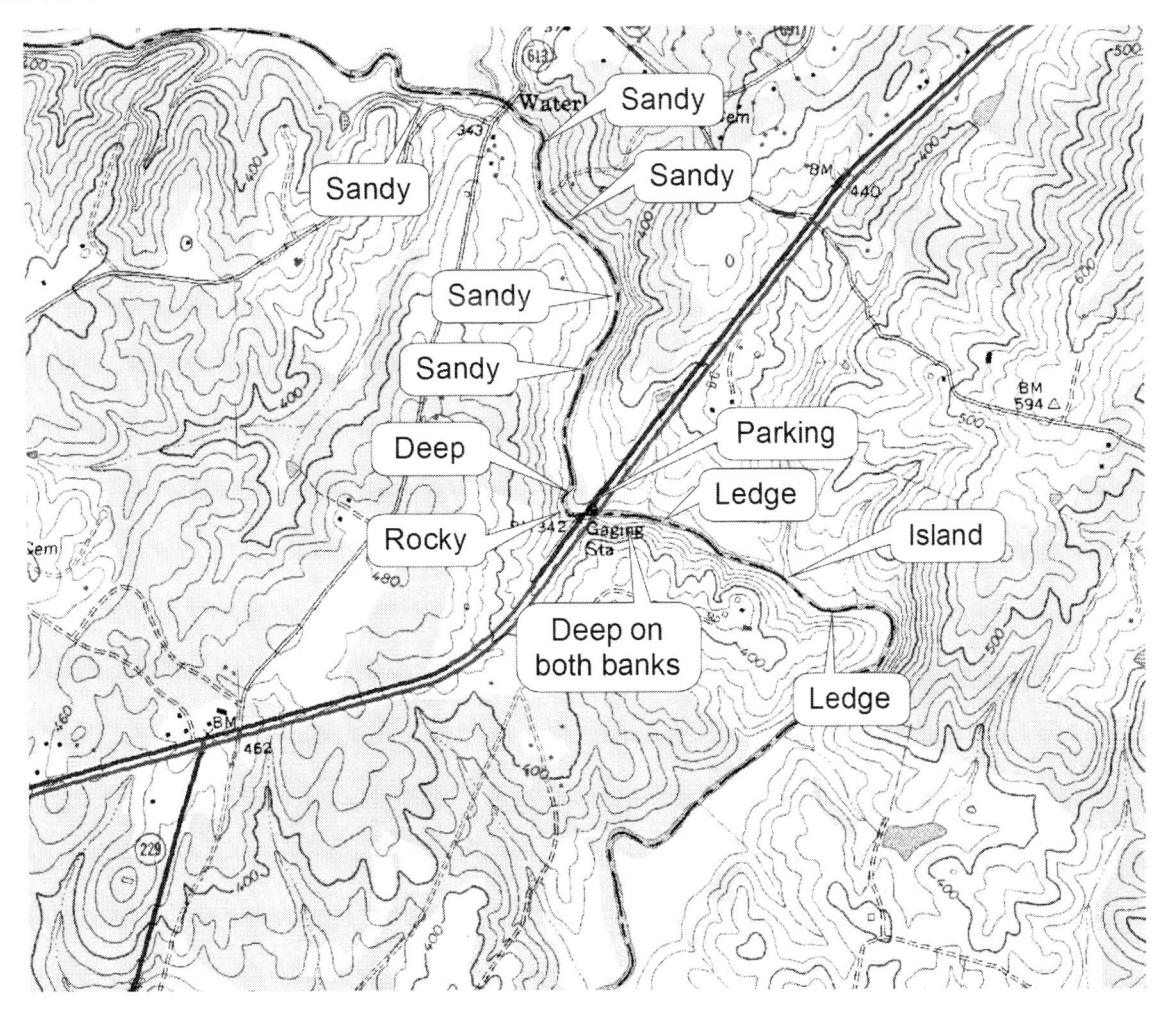

It is amazing how much sand accumulated upstream. Geographically, the river is captured in a broad, level valley where it winds its way through countless farms. As a result, the water loses the velocity it had streaming out of the Blue Ridge and now pushes lazily towards Kellys Ford.

Upstream

After fishing the deep area underneath the bridge, hug the right bank to move upstream. Throw towards the deep water on the left bank. The first bend protects a fairly deep hole that gives up its depth a short distance upstream. Beyond that spot, the river picks up speed as it tumbles down the shallow, cobble-strewn streambed from its source at a small gradient break marking a small lake (38.684851,-77.904022).

Upon reaching the narrow gap that defines the tail of the lake, note that the deep area is bordered by a tight collection of rocks and trees. Move to the right to fish into the deep water as well as continue upstream. The left bank is not wadeable at normal levels. Enjoy this spot since it is the only "decent" fishable water upstream from the bridge.

Twenty yards beyond the gradient break, the river plays a cruel trick and totally destroys any optimism created by the good rocks leading up to the lake. The river switches to sand - endless sand. Even worse, it runs inches deep and does not even try to offer up a deep pool. The sand continues all the way up and beyond the bridge at Waterloo (38.695896,-77.906061). Obviously, that makes fishing from the Waterloo VDOT easement a waste of time as well. While there may be some bad spots farther downstream, this one has to be at the top of the list of miserable places. Granted, it is worth taking the short walk up to the lake at the head of the riffle, but do not wade beyond that point.

The water runs with enough depth to hide the rocks near the bridge at 382 cfs. Do not let that keep you from fishing the short upstream section that leads into the bend.

This is the view upstream at the top of the gradient. Even though the bottom is sand, there is enough depth to make it interesting. Skinny around to the right, targeting the left as well as the log on the right.

The view downstream to the break shows the good structure that clusters at the top of the bend where the river takes a small drop as it flows into the bridge.

Beyond that point, the river is nothing but shallow and sandy. At summer levels, it is ankle-deep.

Downstream

To fish downstream, you have to start upstream. You cannot wade downstream along the left bank as a result of the deep hole immediately under the bridge. Instead, go upstream and cross where it is shallow at the bend. Walk down the shoreline along the right bank, fish the bridge and then slide onto the large sandbar that stretches parallel with the direction of flow. Use the sandbar as your highway.

Fish both sides of the river, targeting the log on the left as well as the rocks on the right. After running beyond the rocks, the river deepens slightly and remains wadeable in the center. Continue downstream working both banks. After passing the rocks, slip right because the river deepens on the left. Throw to the deep left bank all the way down to the leaning cluster of trees on the right. Immediately downstream of the tree complex, there is a small gradient break where the river transitions from sand to rock. There are a few boulders in the tailwater ahead of the gradient break, but, to save time, skip down to the bottom of the break (38.68379, -77.89961). At this point, you are a half mile from your vehicle and are about to fish the best hundred foot section of the river downstream from the parking lot.

Above the break, the water runs across a short rocky stretch, pooling on the left before splitting around a grass island. You can move downstream on either bank. Wander out onto the grass island to fish the deep pool on the left just downstream of the break. On the right, it shallows out – particularly in low water.

0.75 miles into your fishing hike (38.68261, -77.89725), the river tightens up but retains the sandy bottom with a marginal redeeming feature being an increased number of boulders. Continue to wade down the center of the river, throwing at anything that looks deep. The river will remain shallow until it reaches a large rock on the right that channels the water to a fallen log spanning the river (38.682734,-77.897343).

There is a deep section immediately downstream of that log. Move around the log on either bank and take the time to fish adjacent to it. Following that, the river returns to being a dead zone with a sandy desert bottom and runs very shallow to another grassy island complex where the river splits (38.68219,-77.895682). Walk around to the right since there is a pool on that side.

Downstream from this point, the river gets a little bit better as it moves into a rock cliff area on river right. There is good boulder structure and deep water as the river makes the bend to the left and heads into another gradient break (38.681316,-77.894227). It is worth spending time to fish this carefully. At this point, you are a mile away from the parking area and, if the current is strong, you should turn around and slog back out.

Start fishing under the bridge.

Even though it is sandy near the overhanging tree, there is a good rocky bank just beyond it.

The bottom of the first break features a deep pool on the left just beyond the grass at 382 cfs.

When you see the fallen log and the large rock on the right, get ready to fish the deep area just downstream.

This is the end of the hike downstream.

The grass island splits the river with the best fishing being underneath the trees to the right.

There is not enough current flowing in the left channel to make it interesting to anything other than sunfish.

Bottom Line

The downstream run offers up some decent fish. Do not go beyond the first small lake upstream.

River above Lee Highway

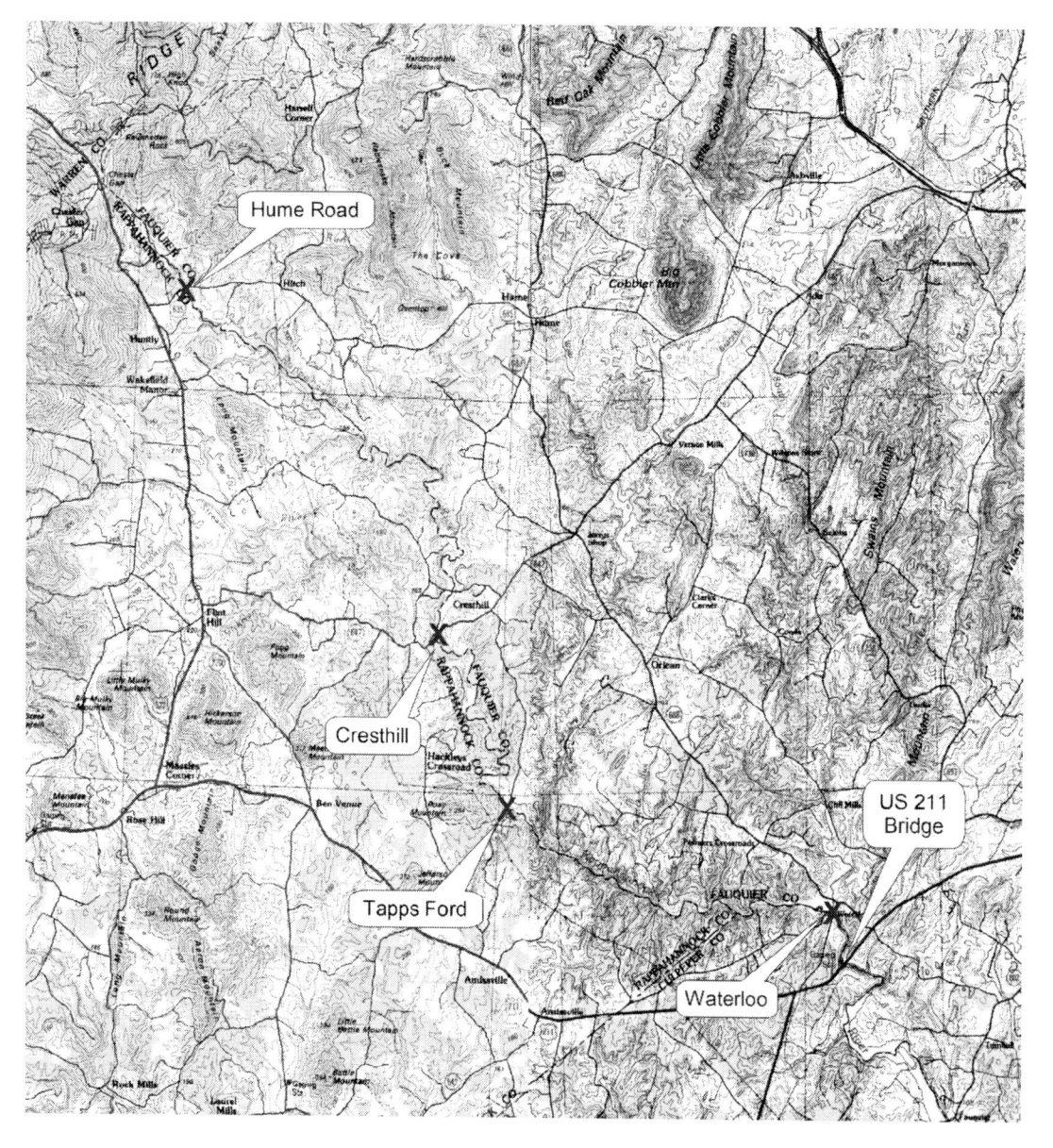

Above Lee Highway, the river becomes small and tight with a uniformly sandy bottom. Beyond that, there is the uncertainty over whether the public may use the streambed. According to my government sources, who declined go on record, there is actually no doubt about this at all – but the fact that they would not go on record makes me believe that there may be some lingering controversy or that the topic is just too touchy.

Therefore, since all of the documentation explicitly calls out the area from the US 211 bridge downstream as being public and is silent on the upstream section, you run a risk of trespassing if you fish from access points above the US 211 bridge. Unfortunately, I cannot give an unambiguous answer. Given the limited road network in the area, there are only five potential access points. Waterloo, Hume and Black Rock Ford should be written off immediately leaving the uncertainty focused on the Tapps Ford and Crest Hill Road.

If you decide to fish at these spots, you are on your own since nothing in this book should be interpreted as encouraging you to trespass. I have not fished at any of these locations and relied on fishing kayakers, who are less risk averse than I am, for their assessment of the water.

Waterloo

Google Map Coordinates: 38.695885,-77.906113

Directions: From I-66 westbound, take exit 43B onto US 29 (Lee Highway) south towards Warrenton. Take a slight right at US 15/US 29 Business south and follow it to make a right turn onto US 211 W at Frost Avenue.

Follow US 211 to the intersection with VA 688 on the east side of the Rappahannock. Turn north onto VA 688.

Turn left on VA 613 (Jeffersonton Road) and follow it to the bridge over the river (38.695885,-77.906113). You may be able to park at the intersection of Old Bridge Road and Waterloo Road (38.695395,-77.906837 - picture).

This picture was taken looking east from the only logical parking spot.

Beyond Lee Highway   169

Totally miserable, totally sandy – not worth an instant of your time (382 cfs).

This picture is not informative given the blockage of the tree. In the eBook, you can see the brown sheen of the sand glimmering through the leaves.

Comment: The land bordering the bridge is heavily posted. Even though the VDOT easement is still valid, it is not worth using it to reach the river. Sand continues downstream to the US 211 bridge and upstream offers similar nonproductive fishing water.

Tapps Ford

Google Map Coordinates: 38.719265,-78.006768

Directions: From I-66 westbound, take exit 43B onto US 29 (Lee Highway) south towards Warrenton. Take a slight right at US 15/US 29 Business south and follow it to make a right turn onto US 211 W at Frost Avenue. Go across the river and continue west on US 211 to VA 645 (Poes Road).

Turn right onto Poes Road (north). Poes Road turns into Hackley Mill Road. Follow it to the bridge (38.719265,-78.006768). There is no parking in the immediate vicinity of the bridge. The road that leads to the bridge from the south runs through a sharp, steep cut with no shoulder.

The north side of the bridge is elevated above the level of the land with a marginal turn off across from the driveway that leads to the home on the northwest side of the bridge.

The view upstream from Tapps Ford reveals a sandy bottom with a few rocks along the west bank (382 cfs).

Downstream looks better as the river runs across a rocky bottom that persists for a short distance downstream.

Comment: Tapps Ford is a well-known put-in for canoes and kayaks. However, access to the river for that purpose is obtained by first requesting permission from the landowner on the northern bank of the river. Granted, the VDOT access continues to exist and, theoretically, you could walk along the road to reach the river if you can find a safe place to park. Those who floated downstream from this point comment that the fishing becomes decent approximately 2,000 feet downstream from the bridge. Therefore, to be on the safe side, I recommend you ask for similar permission to park your vehicle and fish.

Crest Hill Road

Google Map Coordinates: 38.759204,-78.027992

Directions: From I-66 westbound, take exit 27 onto VA-55 E toward VA 647/Marshall. Turn left at VA 721 (Free State Road) followed by a right onto VA 647 (Crest Hill Road). Continue on Crest Hill Road for just under 12 miles to the bridge over the Rappahannock (38.759204,-78.027992). There is a small turnout on the south side of the bridge that has a beaten trail leading to the river's edge.

You can park at the point on the west side where this picture was taken.

The upstream view reveals sand that stretches all the way up to the Jordan River (382 cfs).

Downstream is no better with sand into the distance. The river has no energy here.

Comment: There appears to be plenty of water in the river when you look at it from the bridge because the junction of the Jordan River with the Rappahannock is a short distance upstream. North from that confluence, both rivers become narrow and skinny. According to the VDGIF, the Jordan River is the downstream boundary for the existence of trout. Upstream from the confluence, you might come across a trout or two if the water is able to remain cold enough. Since the VDGIF does not stock trout anywhere in the Rappahannock complex, anything you encounter will be wild. Like Tapps Ford, Crest Hill is a well known and well used kayak put-in. According to kayakers, it is not worth fishing.

Hume Road

Google Map Coordinates: 38.837735,-78.105755

Directions: From I-66 westbound, take exit 18 towards Markham. Turn left on VA 688 (Leeds Manor Road) followed by a right onto VA-55 W (John Marshall Highway). Turn left on VA 726 (Fiery Run Road) and stay on it until it hits a "T" intersection with VA 635 (Hume Road). Turn left (west) and follow Hume Road to the bridge.

Upstream at Hume, the river is a small trout stream (382 cfs).

Downstream shows the same story as upstream. My personal belief is that this is off limits.

Comment: It is hard to believe that the trickle of water that bubbles under the bridge is actually the mighty Rappahannock. It does not even require a hop, skip and a jump to cross the river at this point – a hop and skip will do just fine. Anything in this section has to be trout water. From the bridge crossing, it is the typical mix of rocks and boulders expected given its proximity to the Blue Ridge. Given the fact that the courts look to various navigability standards to separate private and public ownership, there just is not enough water here for me to believe it is public. Therefore, do not attempt to fish here.

Black Rock Ford Road

Google Map Coordinates: 38.845642,-78.112976

I include this to be comprehensive. I know there are folks out there who will do exactly what I did and trace the river upstream to its source, looking for every public road crossing to exploit the VDOT easement. The river dribbles underneath Black Rock Ford Road. Unfortunately, the road leading to this spot is private with no public access.

Shad!!

Google Map Coordinates: 38.319139,-77.468108 to 38.326796,-77.503096

Getting to the Stream

Lower End (US 1 Bridge):

North: From I-95, take exit 133A onto US 17 towards Falmouth. Turn right at the intersection with US 1. Go across the bridge and turn right on Hanson Ave followed by another right on Woodford St. At the intersection with Caroline, turn left and park along the road or go right, under the bridge and take another right on Freedom Lane to park in the lot across from the VFW building.

South: From I-95, take exit 130A onto VA 3 towards Fredericksburg. Merge onto US 1 North and follow it to the bridge. Immediately prior to crossing the bridge, turn right on Princess Anne Street followed by a sharp left onto Freedom Lane. Park in the lot on the left or continue down to Caroline Street to turn left and park on the side of the road.

Upper End (I-95 Bridge):

North: From I-95, take exit 133A onto US 17 towards Falmouth. Turn right at the intersection with US 1. Go across the bridge and turn right on Hanson Ave followed by another right on Woodford St. At the intersection with Caroline, turn left and follow Caroline to the Friends of the Rappahannock property on the river side. Immediately after passing the Friends property, pull into the small parking area on the left side of the street (38.316508,-77.485821).

South: From I-95, take exit 130A onto VA 3 towards Fredericksburg. Merge onto US 1 North and follow it to the bridge. Immediately prior to crossing the bridge, turn right on Princess Anne Street followed by a sharp left onto Freedom Lane. Continue to Caroline Street and make a left to follow Caroline to the Friends of the Rappahannock property on the river side. Immediately after passing Friends property, pull into the small parking area on the left side of the street (38.316508,-77.485821).

To find the river, go across the street, through the gate and follow the road next to the canal to the water at 38.321155,-77.489727.

Shad Fishing 101

Up until now, I have religiously avoided lecturing on smallmouth bass fishing techniques since there are more qualified experts like Ken Penrod and Harry Murray who have written the exceptional books that fully cover that subject. Back in 1975, C. Boyd Pfeiffer devoted 177 pages to educating the angling public on the ins and outs of shad fishing in his simply titled book, *Shad Fishing*. Unfortunately, that book is out-of-print and is only available on the used book market. John McPhee wrote an epic 368 pages in his book, *The Founding Fish*, on the same subject. Unlike *Shad Fishing*, McPhee's book is in print and available for the amazing price of $16.00 (in late 2010). If you want to know more than what I outline below, I recommend you pick up either book. I apologize for the heresy, but the basic technique of shad fishing is not complicated. Granted, Amazon lists 37,421 books on fishing, to include my own, that all argue that there is much more to know and understand to be effective on the water. So, I beg your indulgence.

I was a late convert to shad fishing since I focused on trout in the early spring when the shad run occurs. On a chilly early April morning a few years ago, one of my fishing buddies drug me down to stand shivering underneath the US 1 bridge in Fredericksburg and introduced me to this tough fish. Once you hook up with one, you are instantly addicted and no longer cold. Routinely called "the poor man's tarpon", these guys are hard fighters whose nasty disposition is the edge used to catch them. The basic psychology of the shad is simple. They are not interested in eating. The only reason they are in the river at all is to go upstream to spawn. Here are the bottom-line basics:

- The shad run on the Rappahannock occurs between late March and early May. If the cherry trees are in bloom, the shad are running
- Shad are not interested in eating until after they spawn.
- The only reason a shad will hit your lure is because it aggravates them or distracts them from their upstream journey.
- When moving, shad stay in the current because the current tells them the path to follow to reach the spawning grounds. Fish the edges of the strong current and ignore side channels.
- You can find shad in the eddies off the main current where they hold before making a rush to the next holding spot upstream. Shad prefer deep water over shallow.
- Judging depth is critical for success. You may have to vary the weight of your terminal tackle to get the lure to the right place in the river. Make adjustments until you start to catch fish.
- Cast horizontally across the current and let your lure sweep downstream. Twitch it every once in a while to give it some life.
- The best time is early morning or late afternoon. Shad seem to also enjoy running on cloudy or rainy days.
- Lure selection is not complex. Anything colorful will work with the preference being shad darts. Fly rodders should use streamers that reflect a similarly bright color palette. My personal favorite colors are red/white, orange/white, and chartreuse.

Environment and Fish

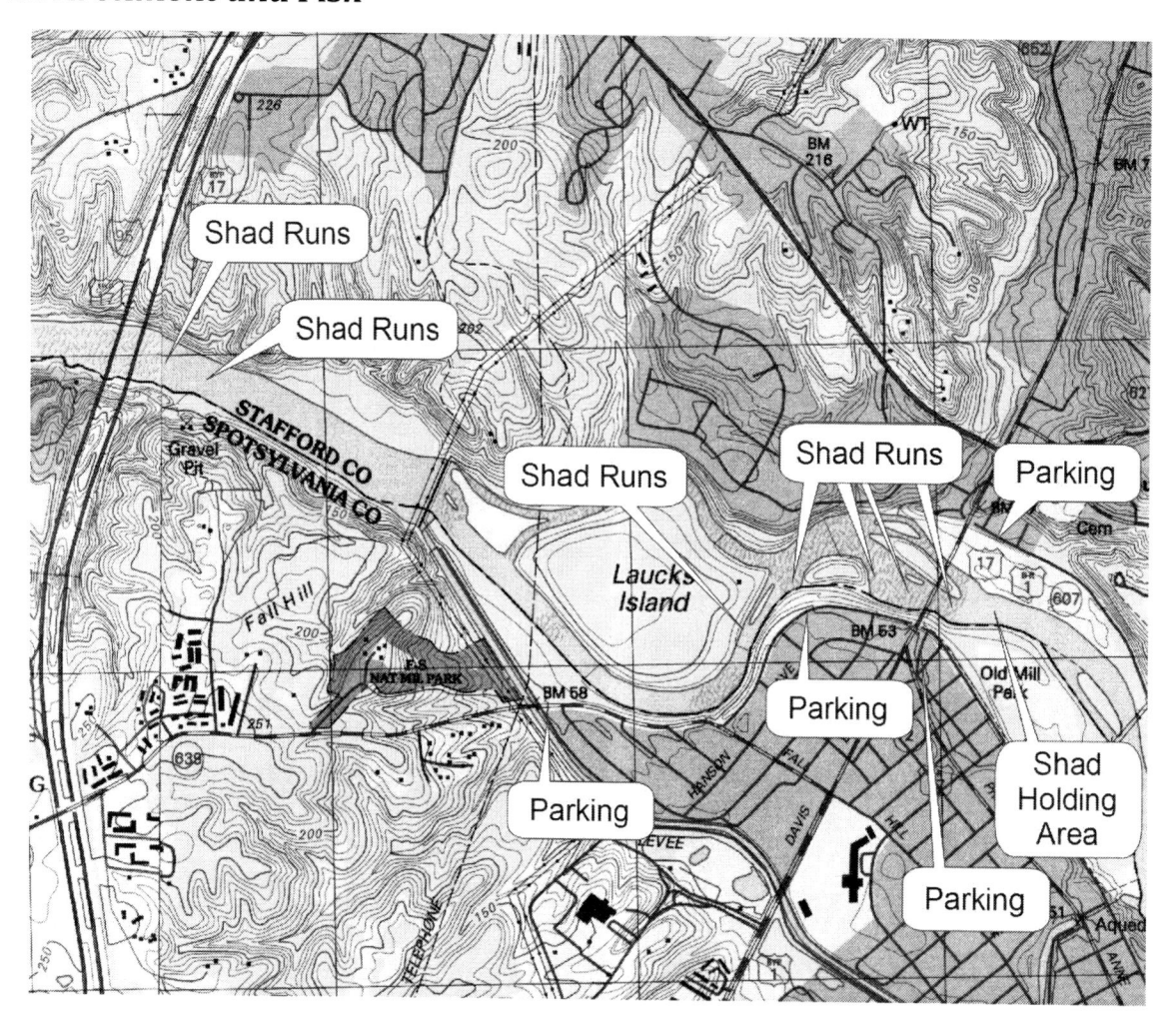

Even though shad have been seen as far upstream as Kellys Ford after the destruction of the Embry Dam, the primary location to pursue this species is Fredericksburg. The most popular spot is the area around the US 1 bridge, but those who are willing to walk a little bit can move away from the "combat fishing" environment of shoulder to shoulder anglers clustered there to have a reasonably solitary experience.

Since shad follow the current, to be effective in catching them, you must follow the current as well. Here are the key places you should target.

- The bend in the river off of Old Mill Park where the water is deep against the northern bank (38.316581,-77.463517). Wade out from the edge of the Park and throw into the deep channel.
- Walk to the northern tip of Old Mill Park and climb down onto the rocks that jut into the river between 38.319169,-77.469573 and 38.319136,-77.468168. The line between those two points defines the deep water that is also in the main stream of the current. You can reach the same spot from the north bank by parking in the Falmouth parking area.
- The channel to the north of the first bridge pylon is good.
- The next deep channel is off of Mill Island. Access it from the Riverside Drive and walk across the concrete wall at 38.320185,-77.475071. The good run is between 38.320419,-77.473323 and 38.320909,-77.47362.
- Off of Riverside Drive and an easy walk down the grassy hill, is the entire channel from the rapids at 38.320192,-77.476493 near the upper tip of Mill Island extending upriver to the major line of rocks running across the river at 38.3181,-77.478172.

Above this last spot, the fish spread out across the 150 foot width of the river and are difficult to target. In addition, the river runs fairly shallow between that location and the collection points below the I-95 bridge. The fish will move quickly through the shallow water to find the deep holding positions below the lines of rapids. Therefore, if you are willing to hike up to the I-95 bridge, that becomes the next place to target this species. Walk up to the bridge. There are two key locations where the fish will hold as they work through the dense rock garden below the bridge. The first is the deep pool immediately below the tall rocks that run across the river at 38.325286,-77.496872. There is a deep pool on either side of this rock formation that will hold fish. Use extreme caution to target this particular location since the river usually runs full in the Spring and it may be difficult to reach the top of the large rock that provides the best vantage point.

Easier to get to is the next chokepoint upstream. Throw your eyes upstream from the tall rock formation to the next line of rapids upstream at 38.325679,-77.498112. If you can fish the pool (access may be tricky if the water is high) that defines the downstream boundary, you can usually find some shad there.

The final spot is immediately upstream of the bridge where there is a large triangular rock formation that spreads its bulk from north to south along the line of 38.326435,-77.503758 to 38.3269,-77.502446. Immediately to the north of the formation is a deep, thirty foot wide channel that is the only way for the fish to move upstream. If you are here early in the morning or late in the afternoon when the fish are moving, you may be able to catch a fish on almost every cast. Since it involves a mile walk to reach this point, you should be alone on most days.

There are always plenty of anglers under the US 1 bridge - stake out a spot early (1,420 cfs).

Even though it is crowded near the bridge, the river narrows - forcing the fish to run the gauntlet. You can pick up some nice ones.

The next spot up is the wide channel that parallels the southern shore leading into the bridge.

It usually has a crowd as well (both pictures at 1,250 cfs).

At the other end of Mill Island, it is easy to walk down the grassy hill leading to the river. Unfortunately for fly rodders, there is no room for a backcast here, leaving this the domain of spin fishermen.

It can be risky to walk the shoreline. Be careful. Note the high water level as measured against the tree trunk in the center. This is typical for shad season.

The I-95 bridge is dramatically less crowded. If you can work out onto the ledge, it is easy to target the compressed channels the shad have to negotiate (1,250 cfs).

I took this picture on the same day I grabbed the shots of the crowds downstream. This solitary angler owned the entire river near the bridge. If you are willing to walk, you can be alone. Also, where he is standing is a great spot.

Shad!!

Gear Guide

Fishing for either smallmouth bass or shad on the Rappahannock does not require any specialized gear. What you use for one, you can use for the other. You probably have everything you need right now, even though I subscribe to the theory that if you know how many fishing rods you have, you do not have enough - a philosophy that can get you in trouble with a non-fishing spouse/partner. Compare what you currently own with the recommendations below and if it is close enough, then you are good to go and can save your relationship.

As I developed my recommendations, I looked for the best value. However, I need to admit up front that I'm not an expert. I do not have a laboratory full of equipment where I conduct extensive tests on every aspect of each piece of equipment mentioned. Rather, this is what I use after fishing for over 50 years on a limited budget. I need to qualify "limited budget." There is a minimum set of requirements that gear needs to meet to give years of reliable service. Otherwise, you will end up replacing it time and time again. Therefore, I will not recommend the economical starter kits found in many major department stores because I assume that anyone who reads this book has already decided that they enjoy fishing and will have moved beyond that level of gear. The starter kits are an inexpensive way for novices to test the waters and assess their enjoyment of the sport - but not a good baseline for years of hard use.

Fly Fishing

As a general statement, I am an avid supporter of the gear designed and manufactured by Fly Fishing Benefactors (FFB), an Internet only retailer (www.flyfishingbenefactors.com). In addition to producing high-quality gear at a very reasonable price, this company donates a considerable amount of their gross profit to various charitable organizations. FFB has manufactured branded gear in support of Project Healing Waters, a group dedicated to rehabilitating disabled veterans, the Virginia Fly Fishing Festival and others.

That said, if you prefer to buy from a traditional brick-and-mortar fly shop like Urban Angler or a "big box" operation like Bass Pro Shop, Green Top, Gander Mountain, LL Bean or Orvis, take this list and use it as a guide.

The minimum weight rod you should use for smallmouth is a 5/6wt that is over 8 feet long. The Rappahannock routinely produces monster smallmouth bass that can exceed 20 inches in length. However, given the expense associated with moving to a 7/8wt rod/reel/line, I do not recommend it unless you need that size rod for some other purpose. Granted, bigger fish demand bigger lures and bigger lures require thicker line that is thrown by a heavier weight rod. Besides, with all the sunfish and smaller bass that will slam into your fly, you will have more fun using lighter gear.

The FFB 5/6wt San Juan rod represents a tremendous value. It matches up against the rods by major manufacturers and is made out of better quality graphite. The San Juan uses IM8 graphite that is lighter and stiffer than the IM6 normally used in rods at this price point ($140 in late 2010). What is the advantage of the better graphite? Fly Anglers Online had the best explanation (my bold):

"When you increase the modulus of the graphite, you increase the ability of that graphite to store and release energy. You also increase the speed that the rod releases the stored energy. That in turn, increases the line speed that is generated in the cast. Increase **the modulus, and you increase the reaction speed and power of the rod blank**.

Unfortunately, increased modulus results in increased costs. The process involved in creating higher modulus graphite is a costly one. The highest modulus graphite material costs as much as ten times more than standard graphite."

Given that, it is amazing that FFB can upgrade everyone to IM8 quality graphite and keep the cost as low as they do. Everything else about a fly rod is just looks since most of the other components are fairly standard. That said, the FFB includes upgraded Portuguese cork, a walnut seat and aluminum lockups.

Once you have your rod, you need a decent reel tuned to the rod. The reel should hold the appropriate weight fly line, with backing, matched to the rod and balance when you hold it at the grip. Your arms will be sore after a full day of fishing with an out-of-balance rod/reel combination. No matter how fancy a reel gets, all it does is hold line. It will be a rare and exciting day if you get a fish "on the reel" and actually have to use the drag. Therefore, choosing a reel boils down to how light do you want it to be and how much money do you want to spend?

FFB manufactures several lines of reels. The inexpensive, lightweight Deschutes II reel offers great looks at an exceptional price. It roughly compares with the mid-arbor from another major manufacturer in terms of performance with the "major" being slightly lighter at the expense of a narrower diameter. The larger diameter on the Deschutes allows it to hold more line. Both have centerline disc drags, one-way clutch bearings and glass composite drag surfaces. Having used both reels, the performance is comparable – so go with the best value – the Deschutes. It was running $99 in late 2010.

If you have additional money to spend, you can move up the feature ladder where the reels become lighter and fancier/cooler looking as a result of the additional machining to remove more metal. But the bottom line is that a reel such as the Deschutes II is all you really need. If you really need to conserve cash, FFB has two very inexpensive, low end reels – the Rapidan and the Madison – that run about $40 and $20 respectively.

Shad comment: In the deeper stretches of the Rappahannock, you may find it useful to use an intermediate sinking tip for bass. When fishing for shad, you should start with a full sinking line to force the fly to the bottom. That said, you must be prepared to alter your attack to move the lure to different levels in the water column. If you find the sinking line is taking the lure too deep, back off to an intermediate sinking tip. Shad are not particular and you do not need a long fluorocarbon or monofilament leader. Three or four feet is plenty.

Backup Solution

Unlike the spin rods I discuss below, fly rods are delicate instruments. Regardless of the manufacturer, graphite is only so tough. If you whack a rod on a rock as you stumble to get to that great spot in the middle of the confluence, you could put a nick in the graphite that makes it snap on your next cast. At the end of the three mile hike into Sumerduck or even the short 0.5 mile bushwhack into Snake Castle, you do not want to lose your ability to fish!

Any time you walk farther from your vehicle than you are willing to backtrack if your equipment fails, you need to bring a backup. Since fly reels rarely, if ever fail, all you need is a compact, backup fly rod that can be dual purposed to keep you fishing whether you are hunting bass or trout.

The industry has a solution - the travel or pack rod. Orvis, LL Bean and Fly Fishing Benefactors all have solutions in the 5wt class. 5wt sits perfectly in the middle between the 4wt rod used for trout and the 6wt rod for bass.

A 5wt rod will do just fine throwing 4wt or 6wt line - allowing you to use the reel from the failed rod and not have to haul around yet another piece of backup gear. As of late 2010, the price ranged from approximately $160 for the FFB rod up to $200 for the Orvis version.

The FFB pack rod in a natural setting... the tailgate of my truck

If you do not think you need a backup rod you can carry in your day pack, think again. Regardless of the manufacturer, pack rods are so light that they do not add to the physical stress of a day of fishing and will save your day when the unthinkable happens. Go ahead and plan for the worst and do not get caught flat-footed, staring dumbly at a broken rod tip, realizing you have a mile to walk back to your vehicle for a replacement.

Spin Fishing

If you are a spin angler, your eyes glazed over when you read the advice for the fly guys. Hopefully, you skipped it and jumped right to here. Thankfully, your problem is very simple given the proliferation of good gear at a reasonable price. Unfortunately, just like the fly rodder, your biggest decision will be "how much to spend?" If your adrenaline pumps and the money in your pocket starts to produce an overwhelming itch when you read the latest issue of Bassmaster Magazine, you may have a hard time with the minimum expectations I lay out below. That is fine. The purpose of this section is to stipulate the minimum, not the maximum. Thankfully, the recommended gear for bass will work just fine for shad.

In his book, *Pursuing River Smallmouth Bass*, Ken Penrod's bottom line on the environment against which you must match your gear is:
- Swift current
- Dense cover
- Big fish

His point being that the ultralight gear many people favor because of the more violent feel it gives when playing most fish ends up being inadequate when there is a real beast on the end of the line. Given the aggressive, tough fight in many river smallmouth as small as 12 inches, you could quickly find your drag smoking to end with a pathetic "pop" signifying that your line just snapped off at the reel seat.

The bottom line on a rod is that it needs to be a graphite medium action. I'm sure there are people who will have different perspectives, but I love my Shakespeare Ugly Stik that is 5'10" and designed for six to 15 pound line (model SPL110). Prior to switching to the Ugly Stik brand, I broke several other rods in rapid succession by handling them improperly. As an aggressive fisherman, I'm not interested in gear that needs to be babied. The Stiks have held up well rattling around in the back of my truck as well as taking the brunt of my weight as I routinely trip and slip in the boulder fields protecting the good spots. Ugly Stiks just will not die. The downside is that some more experienced anglers complain that the rods are less sensitive and heavier than other models.

The Stiks are made using a graphite core protected with a fiberglass ("E-glass") coating. Shakespeare stands behind these rods with a five year warranty. I took a quick look over at the Bass Pro Shop review to confirm that most users opinions match mine. Of the 115 reviews posted, 107 were favorable and would recommend the rod to a friend. Although I cannot put my finger on it right now, I remember reading a review in Field & Stream where the editor tried to break one of these rods by hanging excessive amounts of weight from the end. He ran out of weight at 55 pounds and never killed the rod. These things just will not break.

You can get one or two piece Ugly Stiks. I prefer the one piece since I think it is more sensitive. Stiks cost around $30 as of late 2010.

I use Mitchell 308X reels. They have a fast retrieve (5.5 :1) making it easy to impart the necessary action to stimulate fishy interest. The drag may fade a bit at higher settings, but not enough to make me want to spend more money. In addition, the extra spool allows you to solve any "bird's nest" quickly. Finally, the 10 bearing drive makes it a very smooth performer. A Mitchell runs around $50 as of late 2010.

Other

Personal Communications

You will probably not be able to pick up your cell phone carrier at most of the places discussed in this book. You should plan on being out of communications and consider carrying a personal locator beacon (PLB) in case you have an accident. Remember those guys who died on Mt Rainer a few years ago? What about the NFL players on the overturned boat off Florida in 2009? They were alive for plenty of time, but the rescue team could not find them. When I read about these tragedies, it was a wakeup call for me as I routinely fish by myself when I cannot get anyone else to go. Personal locator beacons provide lifesaving emergency communications, but come at a price.

The cost issue reminds me of a conversation in a bicycle shop years ago when I wanted to purchase a helmet for my son and asked for his advice on what to get. The bike guy responded, "Does your son have a $10 head or a $100 head?" Geez...

I bought a GOOD helmet. So, is your life worth $99 bucks? That is what the Spot Messenger PLB is going for as I write this CatchGuide. The Spot PLB also allows you to sign up for a very inexpensive insurance policy that covers the cost of emergency evacuation. Get something.

Radio

The Rappahannock is noisy. In places where it is quiet, you want to be quiet as well. If you spread out, you lose the ability to share what is working and what is not with your buddy unless you have a small FRS radio with you. There are some models advertised as waterproof, but if you look closely at the disclaimer associated with most of them, they are merely water resistant.

The ones that are truly waterproof are more expensive and put themselves out of the running based on that high cost. If you plan on getting wet, you need a radio rated against a standard that is called JIS7 or IPX7. For more information on the rating standards, visit www.hy-com.com/jis.htm. Therefore, I recommend you take the cheapest radios you can find and hope you do not fall into the river. If you make a splash, no big deal – just get another one when they go on sale or have a big rebate. Even an inexpensive radio has a decent range that allows you to stay in touch with the other members of your party. Given the nature of the river, you will not spread out more than a quarter mile, so you do not need extended range. In any case, if you separate much farther than that, you may not be able to communicate anyway – even if your FRS has a range of 20 miles - because of the "line of sight" limitation associated with FRS radios. "Line of sight" means that the radio will only work if there are no obstructions such as hills or mountains between you and the recipient of your communication.

Wild Animals

The Rappahannock is wild... even in places close to civilization. You can encounter bears as close to Fredericksburg as the Confluence! Therefore, exercise the appropriate amount of caution when it comes to wildlife. When fishing in a remote area, I always carry bear spray. I know there are some people who believe that I am nuts for being overly cautious, but I would always rather be safe than sorry. In fact, after an encounter with a large dog when fishing on Great Seneca Creek in Gaithersburg, Maryland, I realized that I need to be prepared for encounters with all sorts of animals. Of course, the day you forget it is the day you need it.

My fishing buddy, Lon, and I were fishing on the Rose River when I got a call on the radio from him telling me that he had just spooked the largest black bear he had ever seen and it was heading in my direction. I reached down to my hip to get the bear spray ready and realized I left it in the truck. I also carry a small air horn, so I pulled it out and bleated out a few loud honks in hopes of warning the bear and convincing it to change its direction. Thankfully, I did not see him, so it must have worked. If you do not want to carry bear spray, carry a loud noisemaker as a backup option.

There have been a number of studies conducted in Alaska confirming that a large canister of bear spray is a better option than carrying a weapon. I need to comment that the laws routinely change related to chemical sprays and before you carry bear spray or other chemical repellents, it is up to you to check that it is currently legal. A good first start is to check the website handgunlaw.us *for an unofficial opinion* and then check with your local authorities.

Outfitters

Rappahannock River Campground

Rappahannock River Campground

33017 River Mill Road
Richardsville, VA 22738

800 - 784 - 7235

www.canoecamp.com
email: canoecamp@earthlink.net

In addition to being the perfect family setting for a weekend of camping, the Rappahannock River Campground (RRC) offers canoeing, kayaking and tubing every weekend between April 1st and the end of October with reservations strongly recommended during the peak season of May through July. As I mentioned in the chapter dedicated to the river where it borders the property, you can purchase a day use pass to fish the spectacular water a short hike either up or downstream from the improved put-in at the base of the river.

There are discounts available to military personnel, seniors, scouts and other groups. Do not worry if you forget something because the camp store carries camping, canoeing and fishing supplies that you can either buy or rent. They also sell firewood and ice. Please visit the RRC website for current pricing.

This is a top spot to fish on the Rappahannock. There is the rock garden a short distance upstream and perfect deep, but wadeable, water a half mile down that holds plenty of smallmouth bass during the hot days of summer.

The RRC is a full-service river outfitter dedicated to making your day on the water memorable. You have your choice of two trips:

Kellys Ford back to the campground   11 miles
Snake Castle Rock to the campground   3 miles

The Kellys Ford trip takes about six hours to complete; 3 hours for Snake Castle Rock. There is no pressure to meet a pickup shuttle at the end of the day since both trips end at the campsite, allowing you to take as much time as you want to fish, swim or picnic.

You do not need any equipment since RRC provides everything you need including a canoe or kayak, paddle and life jacket. The trips depart at 9:00 and 11:00 AM with check-in required 45 minutes earlier. The RRC offers shuttle service for personal watercraft for a fee.

If you want a more relaxed day on the water, you can sign up for a four hour tubing trip that drifts across some class I and II rapids. These are perfect if you are not an "early bird" since the shuttles leave at 12:30 and 2:00 PM with check-in required 30 minutes earlier. The campground will provide the tube and life jacket.

The campground is close to the Civil War battlefields of Chancellorsville, the Wilderness and Fredericksburg. In addition, there are several vineyards within an easy drive and, of course, great fishing as well. The Rappahannock River Campground has 45 immaculate campsites on their 46 acre property.

While in a wilderness setting, the camping is not primitive. Beyond the picnic table and stone fire pit in each campsite, the operation brings civilization to the woods by providing hot showers, a volleyball court, horseshoes and even a short hiking trail for the adventurous.

This is a family-friendly operation and the owners strictly enforce a no alcohol policy as well as control noise by not permitting radios.

Clore Brothers Outfitters

Clore Brothers Outfitters

5927 River Road
Fredericksburg, VA 22407

540 - 786 - 7749

www.clorebros.com
email: mail@clorebros.com

Between April and October, the Clore Brothers offer river trips starting from different access points that give you the opportunity to tailor a day to the type of water, your energy and time available. Currently, the they offer the following trips:

Blankenbakers to Motts Run	7 miles
Elys Ford to Motts Run	14 miles
Kellys Ford to Motts Run	24 miles
Remington to Kellys Ford	5 miles
Clore Landing to Motts Run	17 miles
Raccoon Ford to Motts Run	37 miles

Depending on the trip, the shuttle times vary with the day of the week and the destination. The Clore Landing trip is not available on Saturday with other departure times on Saturday and Sunday being 6:30, 8:00, 9:00 and 11:00 AM depending on the specific trip.

The standard shuttle departure time Monday to Friday is 8:00 AM. During the height of the season between May and June, you should contact Clore and make a reservation. You can do this by giving them a call or sending an e-mail with the information (see their website for details). You do not need to be an experienced paddler since some trips are designed for beginners. In fact, Clore Brothers has a complete rental operation that provides either a canoe or kayak as well as lifejackets and shuttle service. They also shuttle privately owned boats. If you are a beginner, leveraging the use of their equipment allows you to "test the waters" to see if you enjoy this water sport.

One final point about the shuttle. In the chapter about the Confluence, I discuss an area I call the "lower Confluence." You can reach this spot without the long hike from Richards Ferry Road by signing up for the reasonably short Blankenbakers Farm to Motts Run trip.

Once you unload, pull your canoe upstream and beach it on the city property. Walk upriver approximately 500 feet to the start of spectacular fishing with the best water lying only 2,000 feet upstream.

I know a number of people who would pay much more than the $55.00 (2010 rates) for a canoe and all the equipment or $30.00 if you bring your own gear to get access to that water. Once you are done with the Confluence, enjoy fishing back to Motts Run on the short 7 mile float

When you say "Clore Brothers" everyone immediately pigeonholes them as being outdoor activity oriented. While that is certainly true, "outdoor activities" extend to a wide variety of other events that they sponsor. I did not realize this until I was fishing in the river one Friday and noticed a lot of commotion on the shore next to their building. It was a wedding in progress! Clore Brothers has expanded their business operation beyond canoes and kayaks into event management. The event team can do a turnkey operation for whatever event you would like to hold - even romantic weddings on the banks of a spectacular river. They handle all the details including obtaining the tents, tables, chairs, pavilion, bandstand - everything you need to make your event successful - just bring the people.

Beyond weddings, they plan and host events as diverse as family reunions, retirement or engagement parties, corporate retreats, staff meetings and even pig roasts!

Virginia Outdoor Center

Virginia Outdoor Center

3219 Fall Hill Avenue
Fredericksburg, VA 22401

540 - 371 - 5085

www.playva.com
email: voc@playva.com

The Virginia Outdoor Center (VOC) brings more to the table than just being a canoe/kayak livery. Beyond water sports, they offer a climbing wall, climbing classes, ropes course, kayak instruction, guided day hikes and backpacking trips in the Shenandoah National Park as well as themed youth camps. Finally, if you do not want to venture onto the Rappahannock without professional assistance, you can sign up for one of their full or half day guided fishing trips.

The VOC offers a wide variety of river trips including multi-day options:

Hole in the Wall to Motts Run	6 miles
Motts Run to VOC	4 miles
Hole in the Wall to VOC	10 miles
Old Mill Park to City Docks	3 miles
Ely's Ford to VOC	19 miles
Kellys Ford to Motts Run	28 miles
Town of Rapidan to Motts Run	56 miles

The VOC is open Friday, Saturday and Sunday during May and early June. In mid-June, they open Wednesday through Sunday until Labor Day. After Labor Day, they revert to the weekend schedule until closing for the winter. They will shuttle private boats with departure times being 7:00 AM, 9:00 AM and 1:00 PM depending on the trip. In addition to supporting trips upriver, they also shuttle to the tidal section with those departures being at 10:30 AM and 12:30 PM. You should arrive 30 minutes prior to departure time. I personally recommend either the Motts Run or Hole in the Wall to VOC trips since they include some of the best fishing water in the lower section. You can drift across the fantastic rock garden just downstream of the Motts Run put-in and spend plenty of time in the two-mile section centered on the I-95 bridge. If you would rather drift downstream on a tube, the VOC provides options that maximize flexibility. Tube shuttles depart at 11:00 AM and 2:00 PM with pickups at Old Mill Park every hour starting at 12:30 PM with the last being at 5:30 PM.

Beyond the standard offerings associated with floating on the river, the VOC opens the door to a wide variety of other outdoor adventures. If you want to learn how to rock climb, they are happy to teach you either as part of a group or with a private instructor.

Once you master the basics, the VOC can take you on a guided trip into the Shenandoah National Park where your perch off of a cliff offers fantastic one-of-a-kind views of the surrounding scenery amplified by the right amount of adrenaline. They make it easy since they provide all of the technical climbing equipment including helmets and harnesses. Their qualified instructors are also merit badge counselors for the Boy Scouts of America. They conduct a 15 hour course of instruction following the national curriculum on the Rappahannock Rocks with an evening session in the classroom. Camping is available if you want to add that fun to the mix.

The VOC participates in the "Elements to Excellence" program and the VOC ropes course is one of the fun activities that provides a teambuilding opportunity to companies and other organizations. Confidence building is a core mission for the VOC and they work hard to offer programs for youth to get them away from sitting on the couch playing video games. The VOC typically offers three youth programs each summer and these include a mountain adventure school as well as the "Rock 'N Water" or "Water 'N Woods" programs that offer water activities, rock climbing and hiking in age appropriate groups.

Given that this entire book is focused on fishing, I would be remiss if I did not comment on the Rappahannock/Potomac River guided fishing trips available through the VOC. In addition to offering fly fishing instruction with all equipment provided, their professional guide offers half or full day canoe or bass boat trips. Each trip is tailored according to the skill level and desires of the angler. If you do not have your own gear, they provide it for you, making this a perfect opportunity to get on the water if you happen to be in the area on business or vacation without your own equipment.

Water Flow - Fredericksburg

Day	Jan	Feb	Mar	Apr	May	Jun	Jul	Aug	Sep	Oct	Nov	Dec
1	1,310	1,550	1,680	1,660	1,550	1,050	645	478	344	424	510	805
2	1,340	1,550	1,600	1,650	1,480	1,080	612	490	341	441	569	814
3	1,460	1,590	1,700	1,600	1,420	1,060	609	476	350	423	655	868
4	1,520	1,650	1,710	1,700	1,360	1,040	611	485	367	405	629	790
5	1,500	1,650	1,800	1,640	1,430	1,020	640	500	395	385	625	811
6	1,470	1,750	1,860	1,670	1,350	983	622	477	376	386	580	933
7	1,470	1,790	1,900	1,650	1,360	993	634	453	376	380	670	932
8	1,440	1,770	2,100	1,680	1,350	917	595	475	377	381	630	961
9	1,460	1,730	1,990	1,660	1,290	914	556	454	351	375	630	980
10	1,420	1,700	1,850	1,650	1,280	915	513	463	325	394	630	949
11	1,380	1,620	1,830	1,550	1,210	885	534	432	334	405	644	886
12	1,500	1,590	1,730	1,550	1,210	869	534	423	362	379	654	1,100
13	1,370	1,640	1,680	1,550	1,220	845	532	452	333	375	696	1,050
14	1,400	1,700	1,790	1,610	1,290	835	516	515	351	421	659	1,130
15	1,560	1,820	1,840	1,640	1,330	877	521	426	363	384	645	1,180
16	1,470	1,660	1,880	1,760	1,290	837	476	453	335	398	678	1,210
17	1,340	1,610	1,790	1,800	1,190	768	445	409	319	403	694	1,180
18	1,280	1,640	2,000	1,650	1,180	735	471	413	331	399	685	1,110
19	1,300	1,720	1,950	1,570	1,220	811	477	415	380	410	703	1,110
20	1,320	1,700	1,930	1,640	1,170	797	452	428	373	458	724	1,150
21	1,340	1,820	1,860	1,590	1,160	805	499	444	336	474	720	1,100
22	1,350	1,890	1,890	1,530	1,160	743	476	430	301	514	733	1,050
23	1,490	1,890	1,950	1,580	1,180	773	511	413	319	504	682	1,020
24	1,400	1,830	1,930	1,480	1,130	755	588	387	360	499	694	1,060
25	1,500	1,840	1,950	1,570	1,130	686	598	364	362	510	686	1,180
26	1,710	1,820	1,810	1,570	1,060	767	525	352	329	502	762	1,130
27	1,690	1,790	1,680	1,510	1,280	730	536	378	345	572	750	1,130
28	1,570	1,670	1,700	1,550	1,160	753	508	352	369	560	776	1,200
29	1,520	1,580	1,680	1,490	1,100	687	481	357	380	551	778	1,270
30	1,460		1,630	1,530	1,070	659	475	383	384	662	816	1,280
31	1,480		1,550		1,060		504	384		567		1,280

Fredericksburg - Median for 102 years of record in Cubic Feet per Second (cfs)

Water Flow - Remington

Day	Jan	Feb	Mar	Apr	May	Jun	Jul	Aug	Sep	Oct	Nov	Dec
\multicolumn{13}{	c	}{Remington - Median for 67 years of record in Cubic Feet per Second (cfs)}
1	486	631	714	824	690	505	285	158	114	164	208	378
2	583	641	659	900	632	544	275	175	103	168	231	359
3	600	690	680	891	625	527	255	159	125	145	268	369
4	627	675	683	885	594	530	264	183	123	138	282	344
5	645	667	725	845	624	488	271	179	111	136	247	392
6	605	740	798	808	610	490	251	153	111	139	243	395
7	598	741	808	850	650	465	251	149	105	141	269	482
8	613	710	801	780	674	430	243	164	113	143	282	444
9	544	670	800	789	637	434	224	170	100	156	267	442
10	539	669	745	758	605	425	220	164	112	150	260	430
11	593	646	787	722	605	402	207	151	104	143	285	459
12	532	710	753	726	650	378	230	157	99	146	260	500
13	560	678	780	754	664	377	235	148	109	158	255	467
14	563	685	827	778	657	398	205	130	133	160	259	476
15	609	712	865	721	723	384	190	142	133	168	273	484
16	617	680	832	787	678	381	180	134	124	176	278	545
17	590	703	800	773	608	352	169	145	127	174	277	534
18	560	748	816	754	657	368	159	138	120	174	272	521
19	546	745	870	726	600	392	158	137	137	165	269	505
20	550	750	878	748	592	391	154	152	112	160	289	504
21	530	780	924	702	585	342	184	163	116	195	285	535
22	630	736	995	723	594	302	174	160	106	189	285	452
23	620	726	1,060	724	540	340	167	151	116	175	274	497
24	610	686	1,110	724	572	331	238	137	121	193	286	485
25	595	692	990	707	540	308	222	134	125	172	317	495
26	637	702	995	756	582	314	182	120	114	223	344	489
27	717	707	900	733	569	307	190	112	130	243	328	493
28	658	692	804	722	592	300	182	106	150	234	366	487
29	617	623	830	683	566	275	154	110	156	241	397	505
30	648		788	736	534	296	170	110	150	237	368	543
31	658		760		540		160	115		215		452

Water Temperature

Fredericksburg - Daily Average Temperature based on 35 years of data (Fahrenheit)												
Day	Jan	Feb	Mar	Apr	May	Jun	Jul	Aug	Sep	Oct	Nov	Dec
1	39.8	36.4	42.2	50.0	61.0	67.8	75.1	77.0	75.7	63.7	54.8	42.9
2	39.5	36.7	43.0	50.8	62.0	67.2	76.1	77.2	74.9	62.2	55.2	42.6
3	39.0	37.0	43.6	51.1	61.9	66.7	75.8	76.0	74.3	62.5	54.9	42.2
4	38.6	36.8	43.5	51.5	61.2	67.6	76.0	75.7	74.2	60.1	53.0	42.5
5	38.4	37.5	44.2	51.3	62.4	68.9	75.2	75.6	74.5	60.8	52.8	42.3
6	37.4	36.9	43.9	51.2	63.1	70.1	76.1	76.6	73.4	60.2	51.2	41.7
7	37.0	37.0	43.6	51.6	61.4	70.7	76.9	75.7	73.2	59.9	49.8	41.0
8	36.0	36.8	44.0	52.8	63.1	71.6	76.9	75.7	72.2	59.7	49.9	41.0
9	36.4	36.6	43.9	52.3	63.0	72.3	76.8	75.9	70.9	58.5	51.6	41.0
10	37.8	36.9	44.6	52.4	64.3	71.8	76.3	75.6	70.3	58.9	51.6	41.8
11	37.3	37.8	45.2	53.9	63.8	72.0	76.2	76.2	70.7	58.3	51.0	40.6
12	36.6	37.4	45.1	54.4	63.6	72.7	76.2	76.1	69.3	58.5	50.7	40.0
13	36.6	38.1	45.4	53.7	63.0	72.5	76.5	76.4	68.5	58.9	50.8	39.7
14	36.3	38.3	46.2	54.4	62.8	71.6	77.4	77.0	67.2	59.2	50.8	40.5
15	36.2	39.4	46.4	56.0	63.2	72.5	76.9	77.4	69.1	58.6	49.9	39.7
16	36.2	39.9	45.6	56.4	63.7	72.8	78.6	77.3	67.9	58.9	49.1	39.8
17	36.6	39.3	44.7	56.7	64.1	73.0	78.5	76.7	68.1	57.0	48.8	39.0
18	36.2	39.2	45.2	57.6	64.6	72.9	79.2	76.6	68.1	56.5	47.3	39.0
19	35.8	39.3	45.5	58.2	64.1	74.2	78.6	76.1	67.6	55.6	46.9	38.9
20	37.2	39.9	46.1	58.7	65.1	73.6	78.4	75.9	67.0	55.5	45.9	37.8
21	36.6	40.2	46.6	59.6	64.9	73.0	77.9	75.7	66.7	56.2	45.5	37.8
22	36.9	40.9	47.2	58.8	66.3	72.7	76.3	75.2	65.4	56.2	45.6	38.1
23	37.2	40.7	47.9	59.9	66.3	74.1	76.4	73.7	64.4	56.6	46.0	38.1
24	38.2	41.1	47.6	58.0	66.2	74.7	76.7	75.6	64.1	55.1	45.3	39.2
25	37.8	41.2	47.8	58.7	66.4	75.3	76.7	75.5	64.8	55.6	44.3	39.4
26	38.2	41.0	48.3	58.7	66.8	74.7	76.2	74.8	64.0	54.9	44.5	39.5
27	38.4	41.5	48.9	58.9	66.7	75.7	76.5	76.0	64.0	55.1	44.9	39.2
28	38.5	42.8	49.1	59.7	66.3	74.8	76.7	76.2	63.7	54.5	44.1	39.3
29	37.1	43.2	49.2	60.3	66.8	75.2	75.4	75.8	62.9	53.9	43.3	39.9
30	36.4		49.1	61.1	67.0	75.9	75.8	76.2	61.9	53.9	43.2	40.6
31	36.3		49.9		68.0		76.5	77.4		53.0		39.2

If you found this book useful, please consider the other books in the CatchGuide series by Steve Moore:

Wade Fishing the Rapidan River of Virginia
From Smallmouth Bass to Trout
The Confluence to Skyline Drive

Wade and Shoreline Fishing the Potomac River for Smallmouth Bass
Chain Bridge to Harpers Ferry

Trout and Smallmouth Fishing on the North Branch of the Potomac
A Western Maryland River